More For You:

How To Eliminate Debt, Cut Your Taxes, And Prosper In The New Economy

Sean T. O'Hare, CPA

Sean T. O'Hare, CPA

Table of Contents

Introduction: Why Should I Care About Personal Finance?

This is a question that does not often get asked aloud, but should.

People work extremely hard to earn a living, especially here in the early 21st century. Demands are higher than ever on workers and business owners alike to do more with less. Prices for everything from shoes to lettuce to gasoline continue to edge up, even as the average American's earnings stagnate.

Every dollar has to do more and stretch further than ever before. This is why it is critical for people to understand finances.

Much like language, manners, and customs, most people learn everything they know about finance from their parents. Habits, beliefs, and practices are passed from one generation to another.

When a person grows up in a family that places high value on budgets, savings, and managing taxes, they tend to go on to manage their finances effectively. On the other hand, when a child sees his or her parents thumbing their noses at bills, unable to save, and highly resentful of those who manage their money, the child is set up for a life of financial disaster.

Finances are not the exclusive territory of the wealthy. Finances are for everybody.

No matter what a person's income level may be, it is critical to understand how to manage one's money, save, and plan for the future.

Taxes are an undeniable truth and a part of finances.

Nobody can avoid them, no matter where in the world they live. You must plan for taxes; they are inevitable. It is best to accept taxes as a part of life and appreciate the good things that come from taxes; basics such as abundant clean water to drink, electricity at the flip of a switch, clean roads to drive, fresh fruits and meats at the store, and so much more.

This book is intended to give an overview of finances. It is a book for everybody. Together, we will explore the nuts and bolts of everyday finances and taxes in a straightforward way. We're not interested in selling you financial services or convincing you to invest your money with this company or that; our mission is simply to educate, inform, and empower.

If every adult in the U.S. understood the basics of finances, we certainly would not have found ourselves in such a dismal state of national fiscal irresponsibility – the people would not have stood for it! By educating ourselves and taking control of our personal finances, each of us can inch the country and the economy back in the right direction – the direction of responsibility and planning for the future.

Together, we will explore the basics that are modern personal finance. Our objective is to provide you with the information you need to move forward in some of the most challenging financial times the modern world has seen.

Between the covers of this book, we will explore these financial basics:

> Credit
> Banking Basics
> Lending
> Savings
> Retirement
> Earning Money
> Tax Planning
> Tax Debt Relief

We will provide an overview of each of these topics and explain why it matters, in addition to providing need-to-know information, and common-sense strategies to make the most of your hard-earned money.

The topics are geared toward individuals who work for a living, whether as an employee or a small-business owner.

By the time you reach the end of this book, you will feel more confident and ready to manage your finances. It is my goal to help you feel empowered to take control and make the most of your finances moving forward.

Sean T. O'Hare, CPA

Part I: Making It

Sean T. O'Hare, CPA

Making Money

Very few people are born with a "silver spoon in their mouth." Most people have to work. Even those that do not have to work often choose to work in one way or another, though income may not be their primary concern. For the rest of us, income is the primary concern and motivation for working.

When it comes to personal finance, it is helpful to understand the differences between employment, self-employment, small business, and passive incomes. Though each results in money in the pocket, each has unique attributes, advantages, and disadvantages. It is important to understand where and how you make your money, because the IRS treats every type of income differently.

Work comes in a stunning array of roles, positions, circumstances, hours, objectives, and industries. Though people have always worked one way or another, the 20th and 21st centuries have changed the game. Since capitalism ushered in the Industrial Revolution, things have not been the same. The economy has shifted from an agrarian to an industrial one. It is now shifting to a service and technology-producing economy. Every time the economy changes, opportunities emerge to open businesses and fresh, new jobs are created. Of course, some old jobs are also eliminated.

The bottom line is that people have more opportunities to work in fields and industries that personally interest them and utilize their best assets. With lots of hard work, a little luck, and a sharp mind, anybody can achieve respectable wealth from the "fruits of their labor."

This chapter is going to look at the different ways people make money. Because most people have to work for a living, this chapter will focus on the different ways that people work. Basically, you can make money in one of four ways: employment, self-employment, business ownership, and passive income. The next section will delve deeper into each of these methods of making money and clarify the differences between each.

Employment

Working for the man, doing the nine-to-five, whatever you call it, employment means that you get paid to do a regular job for somebody else. As an employee, you are expected to conform to the policies of the company. Not only is the scope of your work defined by the company, but the very processes you follow to perform the job are usually dictated by the company. Employees have little control over what they do, how they do it, where they work, when they work, and how they work. The key point is that employees get security in exchange for compliance.

Employment is also heavily regulated by the government. Employers have to comply with thousands of laws governing employment practices. Employers are legally required to:

Pay at least minimum wage.

Permit employees to take time off according to the Family Medical Leave Act.

Be fair (non-discriminatory) in their hiring practices.

Provide a safe working environment.

Deduct payroll taxes from employee paychecks.

Pay additional payroll taxes and provide appropriate tax forms.

In exchange for complying with company policy and doing a job as directed, you receive a regular paycheck. As an employee, you are protected against discrimination, liability, unsafe working conditions, harassment, and job loss due to military deployment or medical conditions. Another nice perk is that if you lose your job because of a layoff or because your jerk boss fired you for no reason, you get unemployment benefits.

Being an employee also has many financial benefits. A regular paycheck improves credit worthiness. The longer you have been with an employer, the better it reflects on your credit profile. As an employee, you do not have to worry about paying taxes every quarter – the company does it for you. In addition, you also pay a slightly lower tax rate because the company pays a portion of your payroll taxes. Finally, a regular paycheck makes budgeting and planning for retirement much simpler.

Employees also get to take advantage of company-sponsored benefits programs that often include reduced-price health insurance, retirement accounts/pensions, employee discounts, life insurance, paid vacations, sick pay, and more. Though employment is not right for everybody, it is a stable and reliable way to make an income.

Self-employment

Call it freelancing, contracting, self-employment, or owner-operated – it all means self-employment. When a person is self-employed, they literally work for themselves. Self-employed people enjoy more freedom than employees as far as dictating how, where, and what they will do to make money. They are their own bosses. Only their clients and customers can influence how they choose to work. Many people who are self-employed enjoy working from a home office or shop, and maybe even the local coffee shop.

However, there is a lot more risk involved in being self-employed than there is in being employed. If you fail at your job, there is nobody to rush in and save the day. Income varies. For many self-employed individuals it is "feast or famine." If you are self-employed, it is up to you and you alone to get your work done on time, satisfy your clients or customers, provide the tools you need to do your job, and follow all applicable laws. If you do something illegal, you may find yourself facing a lawsuit. People who find success in self-employment are those who have an entrepreneurial spirit as well as the ability to provide unique products and/or services. They also tend to be independent, very hard-working, and comfortable taking on every role in a business. Self-employment is often a stepping stone to business ownership.

The primary financial benefit of self-employment is that you are in control of your income. You do not have to go to a boss and make a case for a raise if you want to make more money – you just have to work harder, work smarter, or find more work. You also get to take advantage of certain tax incentives exclusive to business owners. Some of the most popular benefits are the ability to deduct home office expenses, mileage, and investments in equipment/tools.

Despite the popular deductions, self-employed people also usually pay more in taxes than their employed counterparts. This is because they have to pay the entire portion of their payroll taxes. Most of the burden comes from the self-employment tax, which will be explained in more detail in Chapter 10. Estimated tax is another annoyance to self-employed people. It is paid quarterly, and if not paid properly, could result in hefty penalties, interest, and undesired attention from the IRS.

Small-Business Ownership

It is said that small businesses are the backbone of America. Small businesses employ over half of the country's private workers and generate over half of the country's non-farm private GDP. The Small Business Administration defines small businesses as those that are independently owned and operated, not dominant in their field, and organized for profit. Depending on the industry, a small business may have up to 1,500 employees and generate up to $21.5 million in revenue. Even "small businesses" can be quite sizeable and involved in elite industries.

The main difference between having a stake in a small business and self-employment is that there is more than just you involved. Typically, small-business owners have employees of their own. They may also have to work with partners, shareholders, investors, and other people with a financial interest in the company. In addition, the company has to be licensed by the state or municipality in order to operate. Self-employed workers do not necessarily have to obtain a license to operate unless involved in food service, financial services, or other regulated industries.

Within the family of small business, there are various ways to structure the organization. Every structure has a specific purpose and intent and must be declared when filing for a business license.

Tax Planning: Choose The Right Business Entity

If you choose to take the plunge into self-employment or small business ownership, the type of entity you choose to organize your business in can have significant tax consequences.

Most business owners start as sole proprietors, then, as they grow, establish a limited liability company or corporation to help protect them from business liability. But choosing the right business entity involves all sorts of tax considerations as well. And many business owners are operating with entities that may have been appropriate when they were established – but just don't work as effectively now.

There are generally five ways you can organize your business.

A *proprietorship* is a business you operate yourself, in your own name or trade name, with no partners or formal entity. You report income and expenses on your personal tax return and pay both income tax and self-employment tax on your profits. These are generally best for startups and small businesses with no employees in industries with little legal liability.

A *partnership* is an association of two or more partners. General partners run the business and remain liable for partnership debts. Limited partners invest capital, but don't actively manage the business and aren't liable for debts. The partnership files an informational return and passes income and expenses through to partners. General partner distributions are taxed as ordinary income and subject to self-employment tax; limited partnerships distributions are taxed as "passive" income.

A *C corporation* is a separate legal "person" organized under state law. Your liability for business debts is generally limited to your investment in the corporation. The corporation files its own return, pays tax on profits, and chooses whether or not to pay dividends. Your salary is subject to income and employment tax; dividends are taxed at preferential rates. These are generally best for owners who need limited liability and want the broadest range of benefits. However, the administrative costs and complexities are also the highest.

An *S corporation* is a corporation that elects not to pay tax itself. Instead, it files an informational return and passes income and losses through to shareholders according to their ownership. Your salary is subject to income tax and employment tax (Social Security and Medicare); pass-through profits are subject to ordinary income but not employment tax. These are generally best for businesses whose owners are active in the business and don't need to accumulate capital for day-to-day operations.

Finally, a *limited liability company* (LLC) or *limited liability partnership* (LLP) is an association of one or more "members" organized under state law. Your liability for business debts is limited to your investment in the company, and LLCs may offer the strongest asset protection of any entity. However, a limited liability company is not a distinct entity for tax purposes. Single-member LLCs are taxed as proprietors, unless you elect to be taxed as a corporation. Multi-member LLCs choose to be taxed as partnerships or corporations. This flexibility makes LLCs the entity of choice for many startup businesses.

Let's walk through one popular choice to illustrate how important this question can be.

If you operate your business as a sole proprietorship, or a single-member LLC taxed as a sole proprietorship, you may pay as much in self-employment tax as you do in income tax. If that's the case, you might consider setting up an S corporation to reduce that tax.

If you're taxed as a sole proprietor, you'll report your net income on Schedule C. You'll pay tax at whatever your personal rate is. But you'll also pay self-employment tax 15.3% on your "net self-employment income" (subject to annually adjusted caps, but still 2.9% of anything above that cap). Since 2013, you've also been subject to a new 0.9% Medicare surtax on anything above $200,000 if you're single, $250,000 if you're married filing jointly, or $125,000 if you're married filing separately.

Let's say your profit at the end of the year is $80,000.

You'll pay regular income tax on those profits, of course.

Then, you'll also pay about $11,000 in self-employment tax.

That self-employment tax replaces the Social Security and Medicare tax that your employer would pay and withhold if you weren't self-employed. If you're like most readers, you're not planning to retire on that Social Security. You'll be delighted if it's all still there, but you're not actually counting on it in any meaningful way.

What if there was a way you could take part of that Social Security contribution and invest it yourself? Do you think you could earn more on your money yourself than you can with the Social Security Administration? Well, there is, and it's called an S corporation.

An S corporation is a special corporation that's taxed somewhat like a partnership. The corporation pays you a salary for the work you do. Then, if there's any profit left over, it passes the profit through to your personal return, and you pay the tax on that income on your own return. So the S corporation splits your income into two parts, wages and pass-through distributions.

Here's why the S corporation is so attractive.

You'll pay the same 15.3% employment tax on your wages as you would on your self-employment income. (You'll also pay the extra 0.9% Medicare tax on self-employment income exceeding $200,000 or $250,000, depending on whether you file alone or jointly.)

BUT – there's no Social Security or self-employment tax due on the dividend pass-through. And that makes a world of difference.

Let's say your S corporation earns the same $80,000 as your proprietorship. If you pay yourself $40,000 in wages, you'll pay about $6,120 in Social Security.

But you'll avoid employment tax on the income distribution.

And that saves you $5,184 in employment tax you would have paid without the S-corporation.

The best part here is that you just pay less tax. It's not like buying equipment at the end of the year to get big depreciation deductions. That may be a great strategy, but it also means spending something on the equipment to get that depreciation. It's not like contributing money to a retirement plan to get deductions. That may be another great strategy, but it also means you have to take money out of your budget to contribute to the plan.

Now, you still have to pay yourself a "reasonable compensation" for the service you provide as an employee – in other words, the salary you would have to pay to hire an employee to do the work for you. If you pay yourself nothing, or merely a token amount, the IRS can recharacterize up to ALL of your income as wages and hit you with some very hefty taxes, interest, and penalties. So don't get greedy! But according to IRS data, the average S corporation pays out about 40% of its income in the form of salary and 60% in the form of distributions. So you can see that there's a possibility for real savings.

Types of Income

There is another way to look at income that will help you understand the different ways to earn money. The IRS groups income into three buckets: active income, passive income, and portfolio income.

Active income is money that you earn by working or actively participating in a business. Most people in the U.S. make money from an active income. Active income is what makes the economy work, too.

Passive income is money that you make from enterprise without being actively involved, such as a limited partnership, royalties, licensing fees, or income-producing property.

Portfolio income is the type of money that you earn from your investments, including sales from profits, dividends, and interest.

Each type of income is taxed differently. Active income is fairly straightforward. Passive income is a little more difficult to understand, and portfolio income can be downright confusing at tax time.

Making Money Wrap-up

Though it may seem like a struggle at times, there are lots of ways to make money in this day and age. There is a lot of freedom to choose a direction, and you have freedom to shift gears at any time. Most people are employees at one point in their lives, even if they go on to become business owners or do well enough in the market that they can live off of their portfolio.

The main ways of making money are working as an employee, self-employment, operating a business, or by making savvy investments. There is no right or wrong way to make money, provided you are following the law and paying your taxes. Each type of income has different benefits and disadvantages.

Employees enjoy a wide range of roles, stable income, limited liability, structured work environments, and sometimes benefits packages. Primary disadvantages are that earning potential and freedom to work as you please are limited by your employer.

Self-employed individuals enjoy freedom to work as they please. Their income is limited only by their capacity. Disadvantages are that they can lose everything if they are found liable in a lawsuit, and the self-employment tax structure is not the most beneficial.

Small-business owners have an incredible degree of flexibility and control over where and how they work. Income potential is effectively unlimited because there are so many ways to structure the business. Disadvantages are that small-business owners tend to work long and hard before they reap the financial benefits of their work. Also, stress levels can be off the charts.

Passive or portfolio income tends to be the most desirable of all. Little effort is exerted, yet the money rolls in. With this type income, it usually "takes money to make money," so you need cash to get it started. There are virtually no financial disadvantages to passive or portfolio income.

Part II: Borrowing It

Sean T. O'Hare, CPA

Credit: What It Is and Why It Matters

Every person with a Social Security Number has a credit profile. It plays an immense role in your life, determining your ability to get financing for large purchases like a home or a car. Credit can also play a role in making smaller purchases like furniture, musical instruments, and computers. Even before you rent a home or an apartment, the landlord or rental agency checks your credit to determine whether you are trustworthy. Credit is what gives people an edge or a disadvantage with finances.

Another interesting role credit plays in your life is that it may determine whether you get hired or not, especially in this age of increased focus on compliance in the workplace. Senior-level leadership positions, management jobs, and jobs within certain industries now often require credit checks.

Credit is the easiest way for outside parties to judge and assess your level of fiscal responsibility. While it is certainly not a total judge of character, it does provides clues and insights about you, your spending habits, and your trustworthiness to lenders.

When a person has a positive credit profile, they get to take advantage of special offers to pay for large purchases over time, rent homes with little or no deposit, and qualify for favorable loans when it is time to make a hefty purchase like a home or business. When unexpected expenses arise, a person with good credit usually has several options at his or her fingertips to handle the bill.

A person with poor credit quickly finds that life is more expensive; big purchases are out of reach and they do not have options to handle those unexpected bills. They also have to pay more to get into a rental or offer a bigger down payment on a home. Businesses have to be built from the ground up, or with the help of friends or family, because traditional financing is unavailable.

Credit proliferates itself, with good credit leading to more good accounts and bad credit leading to more bad accounts. When one institution sees that other institutions find you trustworthy, they will be more willing to extend credit, even offering lucrative deals out of the blue. It is best to keep credit in good shape.

Once a person goes down the bad credit path, it can be a burdensome process to restore good credit. Often the bad news will snowball. It may start as a late payment to a credit card, which may lead to all your credit cards reducing your available credit to practically nothing. Then a substantial unexpected expense like a visit to the hospital or major car repair comes up. With fewer options (like credit cards) to pay the bill, the bill may go to collections, which further weakens your credit profile, and so on.

What is a credit profile?

There are two parts to credit. There is a credit report and a credit score. Credit scores are generated by each of the credit reporting agencies based upon the information they have on your credit report. Together, they make up your credit profile.

There are three credit reporting agencies in the U.S.: Experian, Equifax, and TransUnion. Each maintains an independent profile on you.

A credit report details accounts you own or have opened in the last seven to ten years. If accounts are in good standing, the history only goes back seven years. Negatives such as collections, judgments, and bankruptcy can linger on a credit report for up to a decade, depending on how and when they were first reported. Late payments only stay on a profile for three years.

Credit reports detail information on each account such as what type of account it is, whether it is open or closed, the current balance, payment history, and credit limit (if applicable). Credit reports also contain sensitive personal information such as address, most recent employment, phone number, and social security number. Credit reports also report on judgments made against you as well as recent inquiries into your credit report.

Credit reports may only be accessed by authorized parties such as financial institutions, insurance agencies, employers, and other parties to whom you have explicitly granted permission. By applying for credit – and in some cases a job or insurance – you authorize that institution to check your credit. In some cases, an application grants an institution permission to continue to monitor your credit even if you did not qualify or closed the account.

Any business that accepts payments can report to the credit reporting agencies by either signing up to report to each agency or subscribing to a service.

What is a Credit Score?

Credit scores are calculated based on information contained in your credit report. Scores range from 300-850, with 850 being the best possible credit score. Each credit reporting agency has a unique formula to calculate a credit score.

FICO credit scores are the gold standard of credit scores. FICO considers information from all of your reports and is the score used to determine credit worthiness by the majority of lenders. FICO doesn't disclose precisely how scores are calculated, but tells us that your score is generally based on these factors:

> Payment History: 35%
> Amounts Owed: 30%
> Length of Credit History: 15%
> New Credit: 10%
> Types of Credit Used: 10%

Just to keep you on your toes, each person may be rated differently, depending on certain factors that place them into a particular credit "bucket". For example, FICO uses one scoring model for people that have had a bankruptcy, a different model for people that have missed one recent payment, and another model entirely for people with "perfect" credit. In all, more than a dozen different such buckets exist.

Strategies for earning the best credit scores

Make all payments on time. This is the most basic of basic strategies. Lenders are hesitant to loan already; even one late payment could result in denial. One late payment can also drop a credit score by 30-50 points.

Make minimum payments. This applies to loans and credit cards. Every account will have an associated minimum payment. Make this payment every month (on time) to demonstrate your responsibility and credit worthiness. If you can make more than the minimum, you will look even better.

Stay well under your limits. Lenders are leery of applicants with accounts at or near their limits. Keep account balances at 50% or less of your limits for the best scores.

Maintain a low balance or two. Lenders like to see that they will make a little money off of you. They earn money from interest charged to balances, so make them believe in you by carrying manageable balances on one or two accounts. If you have a home or car loan, you are set. Be cautious! Just maintain a small balance that you could pay off in a month or two.

Keep accounts open. Even when you are no longer using an account, keep it open. The longer an account is open and in good standing, the better your credit. Having unused credit, especially for a length of time, also shows financial discipline.

Pay down large balances. If you do have a lot of debt, do your best to pay down the balances. Do whatever you can to pay down balances. One of the key metrics that lenders consider, in addition to the FICO score, is debt-to-income ratio. Focus on debts approaching credit limits first. For example, if you have a balance of $895 on a credit card with a $5000 limit and another with a $2000 balance on a $2500 limit, focus on the $2000 balance.

Open accounts only as needed. Do not fall into the trap of opening accounts just for the sake of populating your credit report. Have a credit card or two that you use regularly and responsibly, then only apply for loans as needed. Trade up credit card accounts for those with benefits or lower interest as the opportunity arises. Do not fall for the myth that "more is better" with credit, because it is not.

The key point with credit scores is to be responsible. Have credit and use it. Do not abuse it or rely upon it to pay for everyday expenses or whimsical splurges. If you cannot buy it with cash and it is not vital to your life (shoes and fancy meals out are not vital), just do not buy it.

Credit should be an enhancement to your finances, not a hindrance. Credit cards and open-ended lines of credit should be used sparingly and strategically. Demonstrate your fiscal responsibility by paying your bills on time and as agreed. For bonus points, pay off balances ahead of schedule.

Improving Credit

Credit scores are not stable, fixed numbers. They change from day to day, week to week, and year to year. As mentioned before, precisely how a score is calculated is a bit of a mystery. If you find yourself with a poor (below 620) or even average (620-690) credit score, you can improve your standings with a little TLC, discipline, and strategy.

Check for Accuracy

The first part of improving credit is making sure your profile is accurate. In the U.S., you can get one free copy from all three credit reporting agencies by visiting www.annualcreditreport.com. You may also order them for a nominal fee from each agency. Another way you can get a free credit report is by applying for credit. If you are denied, you will receive a notice telling how to get a free copy of your credit report.

 It is best to look at all three agencies' reports because each will have its own history. However, if all you can get is one, then start there by checking it for accuracy.

Are all of the accounts listed accurate? Look at limits, history, names, etc.

Are payments reported correctly? If you made late payments, you cannot do anything about that, but you can correct payments listed in the wrong amounts or incorrectly listed as late, provided you have records.

Are there any erroneous accounts listed? (This may indicate identity theft or it may just be a dumb error on the part of the agency.)

Is your personal information accurate?

If there are inaccuracies, dispute them right away by following that credit reporting agency's dispute process. If you see inaccuracies on one report, they are probably showing up on the other reports, so proceed to the next agency and do the same thing.

Make Payments as Agreed

Because your payment history is the most heavily weighted element of your credit score, make payments on time. Also, make sure that you are paying at least the required minimum payments. If you are unable to make payments, you may be able to negotiate lower payments with the lender.

Avoid Maxing Out Credit

Lenders want to see that you are responsible, so demonstrate that by not maxing out your credit lines. Look at credit limits as a giant plate of delicious fresh-baked cookies. It is awfully tempting to eat all of the cookies, but it is also a lousy idea.

If you eat all of the cookies, your friends will think you are a pig and be upset that there are no cookies left for them. You may also feel sick after eating all of them. It is just not a good idea to eat all of the cookies; nor is it a good idea to run balances up to limits. It makes you look gluttonous and unable to control yourself, and it can be rather sickening when those bills start coming due.

Build or rebuild Credit with New Accounts and Regular Payments

There are few things better for your score than a fresh start. If you are looking to rebuild credit or build it up for the first time, apply for a new credit card, personal loan, or line of credit. If your credit is poor or unestablished, you may have to start with a secured credit card or a small, secured loan. Secured means that the credit is guaranteed by a deposit or collateral (like a car) equal to the credit limit.

Keep it simple and use it responsibly. One great idea is to use the account to pay for recurring expenses like utility bills. Make sure you pay the card off every month for six months. At that point, you should be able to trade up for a more favorable account or qualify for a bigger limit.

You may also want to start carrying a small balance month to month to demonstrate that lenders can make a little money by lending to you.

Avoid Too Many Inquiries

If you are in the market for a loan to buy something big like a home, business, vehicle, or a nice toy like a boat, be cautious of too many inquiries. Every time a lender pulls your report, it is documented as an inquiry. Too many inquiries makes you look desperate, which reduces credit scores. If you are planning to apply for a big loan, do not apply for anything for 90 days before you apply for the big one. Be strategic about how many applications you send and act quickly once approved for the best reflection on your credit score.

Credit Wrap-up

Credit is like your adult report card. It is how you are judged by lenders, landlords, and in some cases, employers. You have credit reports and credit scores that help these people understand how risky it is to loan you money, trust you to pay rent, or extend you a job offer.

Credit scores of 700 or above will get you the best offers and allow you the most flexibility as a consumer. Scores below 620 are considered poor and will limit financial options.

Credit scores and reports are not stagnant, they change all the time. Even little things like an inquiry from a lender or an inaccurately reported account can have a significant impact, especially if your credit is on the cusp of being excellent, good, fair, or poor.

For the best score possible, demonstrate responsibility:

Make minimum payments on time; early is better.

Pay off most balances every month.

Carry a manageable balance month to month on one or two accounts – unless you are paying down a car, home, or business loan.

Do not max or even flirt with maxing out limits.

Open only as many accounts as you need.

Be careful of too many inquiries when applying for major loans.

Remember to think of credit as a big plate of fresh-baked cookies: It's tempting to eat them all, but a poor idea for many reasons. It is best to nibble rather than pig out.

By paying attention to your credit, you will experience the best that the financial world has to offer. Good credit is a solid foundation for a life of manageable finances. Nobody is perfect. Most people will have dings and dents along the way. Fortunately, credit ratings change over time and take into account recent good behavior, not just past mistakes. After three years, late payments are forgotten. After seven years, unpaid accounts fade away. After ten years, judgments and long-standing collections vanish.

Patience, responsibility and strategy all play into maximizing your credit for the good of your finances.

Sean T. O'Hare, CPA

Banking

Banks are the cornerstone of modern personal finance management. Banks also play a vital role in the larger economy and the sustainability of businesses. A positive relationship with a reputable bank is a point of entry into the credit reporting system. Well-managed accounts also serve as a gateway to financing for significant purchases in the future or preparing for unexpected expenses.

When it comes to personal finances, banking is fairly straightforward. Customers deposit money into their bank accounts and then withdraw it to pay for life's expenses. Deposited funds are protected by the FDIC (Federal Deposit Insurance Corporation) and in turn banks leverage deposited funds to make loans and investments. When banks are run properly, everybody benefits because:

Customers have a safe place to store and manage money.

Banks can stimulate the economy with loans to individuals and businesses.

A strong economy means bigger deposits, which allows banks to provide more loans.

Types of Banks

There are several categories of banks, though the lines between the different types of financial institutions are less defined than they were in the past. Every bank leverages deposits to make money by offering loans, investments, and other financial services. The most common types of banks that people use to manage personal finances are commercial banks and credit unions.

Commercial banks are those banks that specialize in serving businesses. Some big-name examples are Bank of America, Chase, and Wells Fargo.

These banks also serve individuals with personal checking and savings accounts. They make money by leveraging deposits to offer loans to customers. Many commercial banks also offer credit, investment, and insurance solutions. Commercial banks are often publicly traded and subject to the interests of shareholders and market pressures.

Credit unions appear to operate in much the same way as commercial banks, but they are organized in a different way. They take advantage of a special tax exemption because they are cooperatives – a specific business model wherein members (customers) own and operate the business. These institutions tend to serve the local community and may limit membership to a specific geographical region, employer, or other criteria. Generally, credit unions are more beneficial to local economies than commercial banks because the institutions make loans to local members and businesses.

Accounts to Know

When it comes to personal finance, there are three types of accounts that everybody should know and utilize: checking, savings, and money market. The next sections will offer more detail on how the accounts work, common features and benefits, and strategies to make the most of each account.

Checking

The primary purpose of the checking account is to provide a safe place to keep money. In the past, when a person wanted to pay a bill, they would simply write a check to the obligor and the bank would deduct the money from the account when the check was cashed.

In the modern banking system, old-fashioned check writing is pretty much antiquated. Modern checking accounts typically include a debit card that can be swiped just like a credit card to make purchases and pay bills. Few people maintain a checkbook and register, opting to use debit cards and online bill-pay services to manage expenses. The advantage of debit cards and online bill-pay is that transactions process faster than traditional checks. This keeps account balances accurate and finances simpler to manage.

Checking accounts also allow customers to withdraw funds in cash through ATMs, cash-back, or counter withdrawals. In short, checking accounts are an uncomplicated and convenient way to save and keep track of your money.

Checking Account Strategies

Use automatic deposit when it is offered. On payday, automatic deposit is faster, more accurate, and more convenient than traditional check deposits. Many employers offer automatic deposit as an alternative to traditional paychecks. Automatic deposits are essentially wire transfers made between banks, so funds are available immediately. In addition, signing up for automatic deposits may reduce or eliminate monthly fees associated with the checking account.

Get to know and love online banking. Online banking includes mobile apps. One of the biggest benefits to modern banks is the ability to check your account balance, see recent transactions, make transfers, and pay bills with a few clicks. Do keep in mind that not every transaction will process instantly – but most do. This makes it easy to stay on top of your balance and manage your budget.

Use bill-pay services whenever possible. Most institutions offer online bill-pay service; they write and send a check on your behalf to a specific payee. You can even set the date the check will arrive. Online payments may be processed electronically, which means that they are instantly deducted from the account, making your money easy to track. The best part is that there is no need for envelopes and postage; the bank takes care of that.

Always keep a cushion in the account. It is a good idea to keep a little extra money in the account to cover unexpected expenses or miscalculations. Not only is it frustrating when there is not have enough money to pay bills, but it can also be painfully expensive. Keeping a cushion in the account provides a little extra breathing room and financial flexibility. Financial experts recommend that a sum equal to one to three months' expenses be kept in the checking account. If this is not possible for you, just do what you can. Even $20 - $100 can prevent overdraft disasters and bounced checks.

Opt out of overdraft coverage. An overdraft is a term that refers to a charge that results in a negative balance. Most banks offer overdraft coverage, a service that allows charges to process even if there are not enough funds. Banks are required to allow customers to opt out. The trouble with overdraft coverage is that it is expensive. Most banks impose stiff fees in exchange for covering the expense. These fees are usually about $30 per charge and are followed up by an additional fee of $5-$15 every day the account remains in the negative. For example, let's say that your grocery bill was $80, but there was only $60 in the account. A few days later you notice the account balance is at -$65. The negative balance is the result of the $20 of your bill that the bank covered, + the $30 fee, + $15 because the debt has been unpaid for three days.

Bundle accounts to avoid fees. Many institutions will waive fees for customers holding multiple accounts. Check with your bank to see what types of options are available.

Use one checking account to pay bills, and another to manage everyday expenses. Take control of recurring monthly bills by managing them separately from everyday expenses. Calculate how much is needed to pay the bills and deposit that amount in a dedicated bill-paying account. Hold excess funds in a separate checking account or in cash. When the bills come due, pay them out of the bill-paying account. Use the other checking account or cash reserves to pay for everyday expenses like groceries and gasoline. The money will be there for the bills. You will spend less time trying to figure how much you have for other expenses.

Beware fees. Banks, especially major commercial banks, often charge customers fees to bank. Fees can include charges to access ATMs, make a counter deposit, or monthly maintenance fees. Other fees to keep on the radar are those charged for a balance dropping below minimum requirements, returned-check fees, statement fees, withdrawal fees and more. Read all literature carefully to avoid getting worked over by a bank.

Savings

The primary purpose of the savings account is to save money, like an adult piggy bank. Saving accounts are a convenient way to build up emergency funds or save for a big purchase like a house or car. The beauty of savings accounts is that the funds are fully accessible to the customer, and if linked to the checking account, funds can be transferred immediately between accounts.

Savings accounts also provide the benefit of making you more credit-worthy. Banks are more willing to lend to customers that maintain savings accounts with stable balances than they are to people who have no savings.

As far as personal finance management goes, savings accounts make it easy to separate and manage money. If some of your cash is not needed in the near term, store it in a savings account, where it will be separate from the checking account and generate a nickel or two in interest. Savings accounts are backed by the FDIC and are more secure than keeping cash in the house.

Savings Account Strategies

Protect your savings. Pulling money from your savings account is always a better idea than using credit cards or loans to pay expenses. However, try to find another way to pay the bills that does not diminish your savings account, like negotiating a payment plan. If you must pull from savings, make a plan to pay it back and treat it as a monthly bill.

Make regular deposits or transfers. Just as you faithfully pay your cell phone bill, faithfully pay yourself with regular deposits or transfers into your savings account. Employers that pay via automatic deposits can also deposit a certain amount of your paycheck into different accounts. If there is not much wiggle room in the budget, make the deposit small, like $25. The point is to create the habit of savings. Increase deposits every time you get a raise, earn a bonus, or pay off debts. Tip: Many banks will waive fees in exchange for recurring transfers from checking to savings accounts.

Deposit anything left over after paying bills and monthly expenses. Even if it is just a few dollars, put it in the savings account and watch it grow over time.

Be mindful of how many withdrawals you make monthly. U.S. law requires that banks charge fees when there are more than six withdrawals from the savings account in a month. If you must dig into your savings, pull out more than you need so that you do not have to make excessive withdrawals.

Shop around for high-yield savings accounts. Most savings accounts offer pathetic interest rates of less than 0.1%. If your bank does not offer a suitable savings account with a higher interest rate, shop the competition. Consider minimum balances, deposit requirements, and withdrawal penalties before setting up any savings account.

Take advantage of savings programs offered by your bank. Banks are interested in increasing the size of savings accounts because it enables them to make more loans and therefore more money. A lot of banks offer programs to help you save, such as rounding debit card purchases up and transferring the change to savings, cash rewards for deposits, and more.

Money Market
A money market account is a special type of savings account that is a fusion between checking and savings. Typically, these accounts pay a higher interest rate and also have specific minimum balance

requirements. A customer can write a limited number of checks from the account, which makes them a little more flexible than traditional savings accounts. The number of checks a customer can write varies from institution to institution, though it is normally six or fewer.

The advantage of the money market is the higher interest rate and accessibility of funds. The disadvantages are the minimum balance requirement and limitations on withdrawals. Money market accounts are often used to hold emergency funds separate from savings accounts.

When opening a money market account, be sure to consider fees, how frequently the money will need to be accessed, and interest rate. Choose the option with the least expensive fees, highest interest rate, and most flexibility. Money markets may be held at a different bank from where you hold checking/savings accounts.

Make the Banks Work for You

Modern banking can be convenient, but there are some caveats to keep in mind. The most crucial thing to remember is that you are in control of your money – not the bank. You are the customer and the bank works for you.

If the bank is whittling away your money or playing games when you need it, withdraw your money and find another bank.

Major commercial banks offer the convenience of name-brand recognition, lots of locations, and a long list of financial services. Local institutions like small commercial banks and credit unions offer a more personalized experience, benefit to the local community, and customer-friendly banking services. After the Wall Street bailout of 2007, many people are choosing to bank locally to keep their money in their communities.

Fees are an issue that can make banking quite expensive. Open accounts with banks that offer customer-friendly options like free checking (without any strings attached), rewards programs, free withdrawals at any ATM, fraud protection, and free online banking. Remember, make the banks work for you – avoid fees.

Banks play a prominent role in personal finance because they are the best place to store money. Every checking and savings account is insured by the FDIC, which means that even if the bank collapses, you will not lose your accounts valued between $100,000 and $250,000. Note: The actual amount of FDIC insurance on your accounts will vary based on when they were opened, and how they are affected by the Dodd-Frank Wall Street Reform and Consumer Protection Act.

It is safer to keep money in a bank account than it is to store cash around the house. Even if somebody steals your identity, banks will usually replace the lost funds and stop the thief from doing any additional damage with hi-tech rapid response. In contrast, if a thief steals your cash (or it gets lost) there is little that can be done to get it back.

Banking also makes it easy to keep track of your money, organize savings, and pay bills. Having accounts in good standing makes it easier to obtain credit, especially from the institution where you bank. Savings accounts are a blessing when emergencies happen, or when it is time to buckle down and save for a big purchase.

Though modern banking systems are quite complex, checking and savings accounts are straightforward and simple to manage. Take control of your finances by making the banking system work for you with savvy checking and savings account management.

Lending

Besides being places to hold and organize money, banks also provide another service vital to personal finance: lending. Loans and credit (lending) are one of the main reasons the middle class grew to be so large and prosperous through the 19th and 20th centuries.

It is a vital piece of modern economies. Without lending, real estate would not be developed, startups would never get off the ground, home ownership would be limited to the wealthiest classes, farmers would not be able to harvest crops, etc.

On a personal level, lending allows people to make purchases they could not normally afford – like a house, a car, an education, new furniture, and so on. When unexpected expenses hit, lending is also an option to ease the pain.

For all of the benefits lending offers, it is a double-edged sword when it comes to personal finance. While the relative abundance of credit makes it easy to handle emergencies and make large purchases, debts can be damaging – not to mention expensive.

For some, credit becomes an addiction that eventually leads to financial ruin. It is crucial for everybody to understand lending to avoid financial troubles. With discipline and knowledge, most people can sidestep lending-related problems altogether.

In this chapter, we will take a look at the various types of loans and credit available, how each type works, and vital information that everybody should know. Each section will also outline strategies to help you make the most of lending in your personal finance picture. This section will focus on lending as it applies to individuals, not businesses.

Credit Cards

Ah, credit cards. Few things are more American than apple pie and credit card-funded shopping sprees. Unfortunately, credit cards are one of the most expensive forms of lending. When people find themselves in financial ruin due to debt, credit cards are often the culprit.

Like so many things in life, there are trade-offs. Credit cards are not all bad; they can also be a blessing. When used responsibly they can be quite beneficial. Consider some of the advantages of credit cards:

> The credit is already there; you do not have to apply for a loan every time you want to use it. Swipe, sign, and done!

> They are widely accepted by merchants around the world.

> If traveling abroad, credit cards automatically process currency conversions.

> Many credit cards offer enticing rewards like airline miles, gift certificates, etc.

> Responsible use contributes to a favorable credit score and profile.

> Credit cards allow people to splurge, treat friends to dinner, and be impulsive.

The key is to use credit cards responsibly in order to reap the benefits. This means being careful about running up bills, making payments on time, and not relying on the credit card for everyday expenses.

How They Work

Most credit cards are classified as revolving credit. It is a type of lending where borrowers are not required to pay back their loan in a certain time period, so long as they are making required minimum payments and are within credit limits. Revolving credit can also be accessed over and over again. It is called revolving credit because the debt goes around in a circle like a revolving door.

As the credit revolves every month, interest is also charged to the account. Credit cards carry some of the highest interest rates among lending products and solutions. Required monthly payments range anywhere from 1% to 5% of the balance, and must be made by the due date in order to avoid a negative report to your credit profile.

The sticking point with credit cards is how minimum payments are calculated, how interest is charged, and how payments are applied. In extreme circumstances, minimum payments may only cover interest charges. At rates between 10 and 30%, that interest stacks up quickly.

Another issue to be aware of with credit cards is running up the balances. Even if you just charge a little here and a little there, balances still grow at an alarming rate because of how they are structured. Carrying balances that are too high may impact your credit score and credit worthiness because it impacts your debt-to-income ratio.

Strategies for Managing Credit Cards

Do not spend more on a credit card than you can afford to pay off in a month or two. If a purchase is going to take more than a couple of months to pay off, step back and consider whether the purchase is a want or a need. If it is a need or an emergency, then do what you have to do, but try to find a less expensive option or pony up the cash. Limit want-driven purchases to amounts you can pay off in a month or two in order to stay out of trouble.

Choose your cards carefully. Not all credit cards are created equal. Key points to consider are annual fees, grace periods on purchases, perks/rewards, and interest rates. Avoid cards that charge annual fees, unless you get something of substantial value from the associated perks. Choose credit cards that offer a 25-day or longer grace period, then try to pay off purchases within that period – it's free money (and maybe rewards) when you use credit cards like that! Opt for a credit card that offers perks or rewards. Choose credit cards with the lowest interest rates but keep in mind that the lender can change the rate at any time, without notice.

Be responsible. While it may be tempting to use a credit card to redo your wardrobe, buy new furniture, or take a luxurious vacation, it is a lousy idea – unless you can pay it back within a couple of months.

Always pay more than the minimum payment. If you pay minimum payments, by the time you have paid off your balance you will have paid at least double what you would have paid in cash. It is okay to carry a small balance from month to month – in fact it can help your credit profile – but do not allow balances to build up to unmanageable amounts. Also, make your payments on time!

Calculate the cost of a balance transfer before initiating. Most balance transfers are charged a fee between 3% and 5%. If transferring a balance to take advantage of a low interest offer, the interest savings should be at least double the balance transfer fee. Also, calculate what interest will be once the special offer expires. If it is more than you are paying now, it is probably best to stay put.

Unsecured Loans

Examples of unsecured loans are personal loans and lines of credit. Most financial institutions offer unsecured loans. They may be open-ended or closed-ended.

Open-ended loans are those that you can borrow from repeatedly. Credit cards are technically open-ended loans, though they are most often referred to as revolving accounts. Another common type of open-ended loan is a line of credit.

Closed-ended loans are those that are a one-time offer. The borrower is given the money, has a set amount of time to repay, and typically has a fixed payment plan. Once repaid, the borrower may not access the credit again. Personal loans and student loans are good examples of unsecured "closed-ended" loans.

An unsecured loan is one that is offered in good faith. There is no collateral such as a house or car to back an unsecured loan, so they tend to be harder to obtain. You qualify for the loan based on your credit profile/score and income.

Typically, unsecured loans include structured payment plans and an end date. Interest rates tend to be lower than credit cards but higher than secured loans. Funds can be used for anything you wish. Common uses of unsecured loans are debt consolidation, education, business start-up, hobbies, vacations, and even buying things like cars or home renovations.

Lines of credit are different from personal loans. They are often associated with a bank account and are an open-ended loan. They function much like a credit card, but without a card to swipe. Lines of credit are often used as a security buffer for a checking account. For example, your bank may offer overdraft protection that draws from a line of credit rather than charging the overdraft fees referenced in Chapter 3. There is usually still a fee involved for the service, but it is much lower.

Strategies for Managing Unsecured Loans

Read the terms carefully. Look out for loans that have prepayment penalties and variable rates. Prepayment penalties are assessed to penalize the borrower for paying down the loan early. This should never be a term of any loan you sign. It deters you from doing exactly what you should do with any loan – pay it off as quickly as possible. Variable rates mean that your payment may go up in the future.

Manage lines of credit like credit cards. Keep the balance manageable and pay back funds as quickly as possible. Link a line of credit to your checking account to act as overdraft protection, but do not rely on it. It still costs money in interest and fees!

Pay down the loan as quickly as possible. This should be a no-brainer. Pay your debts back ASAP.

Secured Loans

Secured loans are the granddaddy of all loans. It is the closest thing to barter found in the banking system. Essentially, the bank gives you money, and you give them something of equal or greater value for the cash. When a borrower defaults on a loan, the collateral is taken and sold to reimburse the bank for the loan. This process is called repossession or foreclosure. Secured loans are favored because they motivate the borrower to pay back funds and minimize the provider's risk.

Common examples of collateral are things like:

The house

The car

Adult "toys" like boats and RVs

The business

A lien on personal property

Collateral makes these loans easier to obtain than unsecured loans. Secured loans tend to have the lowest interest rates and most flexible terms. Remember, the bank is confident that you will pay them back because they own something valuable to you.

Though you may or may not like banking practices, it is a fact that secured loans keep the economy going. From a capitalist perspective, it is a win-win situation. People who are not wealthy can make big-ticket purchases, while wealthy people can rest easy that they will be financially rewarded for the loan.

Secured Loans to Avoid

Loans can also be secured by short-term liens on personal property, bank accounts, and paychecks. Payday advance loans and car title loans may not require a credit check, but the fees they charge are outrageous. While there are some reputable companies that provide these services, most tend to be bottom dwellers. Loans like these are the territory of loan sharks and should be avoided at all costs.

Advance-fee loans are a scam. These are the types of loans where the lender will offer cash, but you have to send them a "deposit" to initiate or process the loan. Any potential lender offering to give you money in exchange for money is up to no good. Borrowers rarely see the loan materialize. Stay away from these loans!

Strategies for Managing Secured Loans

Get preapproved. For large loans like a house, car, or "toy," apply for preapproval before shopping. It makes you legitimate to agents and salespersons. It also predetermines your budget. Finally, it gives you leverage in negotiations. Because you essentially have the money in your pocket, you can negotiate a lower price than somebody who does not have funding.

Act quickly once preapproved. Loan preapprovals usually result in an inquiry into your credit profile, which reduces the score a bit and makes it harder to qualify for other loans. If you let the opportunity pass by without finalizing the loan, it may also reduce your credit-worthiness, as it may cause lenders to perceive you as a waste of their time.

Preapproval or prequalification? Find out if the offer comes with a commitment from the lender to fund. Preapproval usually means the loan just needs to be finalized with a purchase. Prequalification usually means the institution is likely to fund a loan. Preapproval usually involves a credit

Sean T. O'Hare, CPA

profile inquiry, while prequalification usually does not. Clarify what type of "pre" it is before initiating the process. Serious buyers need preapproval to obtain leverage in negotiations.

Understand the terms. Before you sign, carefully read the loan documents and ask questions to make sure you understand the details. How is interest charged? Are there prepayment penalties? What happens if you default? What are your options for re-negotiation? As always, stay away from loans that include prepayment penalties.

Pay back the loan as quickly as possible. Debt is always better once it is paid back! Nobody wants to be beholden to another. Pay back the loan as quickly as possible by making larger payments or dedicating a portion of extra income to payments. Even an extra $5 a month will add up over the life of a loan. You will save on interest and improve your credit score.

Understanding Interest

Interest is the cost for borrowing money. It is how lenders make money from loans. Essentially, interest is charged to the principal of the loan – or the amount that was loaned. Successful loan management means understanding how interest is charged, and it is different for every loan. Here are some common ways interest is charged:

Compound Interest: Interest is charged daily or monthly, based on an annual rate. With this method of calculation, the borrower pays interest on interest. This is the model favored by most institutions because they make lots of money.

For example, let's say you have a credit card that charges 15.9% interest and it is compounded daily. The balance on the account is $2,000. That means that every day you carry a balance, you are charged .043% of the balance – or $.86. This is calculated by dividing the interest rate by 365. If it was compounded monthly, interest charges would be 1.33% or $26.60.

Tip: Before committing to the loan, find out how often interest is added to the principal. It is usually daily or monthly. Avoid loans that add interest to principal daily; opt for those that do it monthly. With a monthly interval,

50

you can beat the lender at its own game by paying interest charges before they are added to the principal.

<u>Tip:</u> Find out how payments are applied, especially with credit cards. If the payment is entirely dedicated to interest, you will struggle to pay back the debt.

Simple Interest: A straightforward method where interest is calculated by multiplying the loan by the interest rate and duration. Interest is only charged to the principal, so the costs are more predictable. It is also known as "flat interest."

For example, let's say you have taken out a personal, unsecured loan for $500 to cover an unplanned medical expense. The interest rate is 12.6%. You have 6 months to pay back the loan. Your expected interest = $500 x .126 x 6, or $378. Provided there are no prepayment penalties, you can reduce interest by making payments in excess of the minimum.

Tip: Avoid simple interest loans that pay back interest charges first. Some lenders calculate interest for the life of the loan, then apply payments to that sum before applying a dime to principal. This method is an underhanded way to deliver prepayment penalties. When payments are applied in this manner, the borrower gets NO benefit from paying back the debt early. Do not commit to loans structured in this manner.

Lending Wrap-Up

Lending is a benefit to people who are not born into wealth because it opens the door to prosperity and luxury. Lending is crucial to economies around the world because it stimulates business, funds innovation, and bolsters the economy by keeping cash flowing.

There are many types of loans and credit available. Every loan is different, which is why you have to understand the terms associated with any loan you take out. No two institutions are alike, and no two loans are alike. Every loan is governed by a contract and enforced through the legal system. Common types of lending are:

> Credit Cards
> Unsecured Loans – like lines of credit, student loans, and personal loans
> Secured Loans – mortgages, auto loans, payday loans

Irresponsible use of loans can result in financial ruin. Default is a serious problem resulting in the loss of home or other property in extreme circumstances and inability to participate in the financial system in less severe circumstances.

The penalties for not paying back a loan in accordance with terms will always result in the loss of credit-worthiness. As discussed in Chapter 1, bad credit perpetuates itself. Penalties include dealing with collections agencies, garnishment, litigation, judgments, repossessions, and foreclosure. No sum of money or earthly possession is worth the stress, hassle, and embarrassment that accompany these processes.

In addition, failing to pay back a loan is expensive. Lenders charge late fees, collections fees, and other charges when a loan is not paid back. If you take out a loan of any kind, it is of paramount importance that you be able to pay it back according to the terms. If you cannot, do not take the loan.

Part III: Growing It

Sean T. O'Hare, CPA

A Deep Look at Savings Strategies

Why do savings matter? We hear a lot of fuss these days about saving money for retirement or a house, but what is the real reason you should care about savings? Savings is the key that unlocks the door to financial freedom. Savings allows regular "working stiffs" to live without debt, to do things they want to do, and to leave a legacy for their families.

Savings takes on many forms. For some people it is a pile of cash under the mattress – or so to speak. For the majority of people, their savings is a bank account that accompanies a checking account. Many people are savvy and/or fortunate enough to sit on a retirement account. There are also investment accounts, brokerage accounts, and savings in the form of tangible items like precious metals.

The objective of any savings account is to secure, or at least stabilize, the account holder's future. Savings accounts take on many forms and serve many purposes. People may hold several different types of savings accounts as part of a savings strategy. There are also people who lump all of their savings into a single account.

Though this section will not focus on them, there are many options for people who wish to save in the form of tangible possessions. Precious metals, gemstones, merchandise, and real estate are popular alternatives to traditional cash savings. Most people opt to integrate tangible savings into their total financial picture, as a complement to cash savings and investments.

The most complex types of savings are those that rely upon investments such as stocks, mutual funds, ETFs, and bonds. This section will touch on some of these savings accounts, but not in complete detail. If you are interested in investments, consider picking the mind of a qualified financial adviser.

Understanding Savings Buckets

Savings accounts have many purposes, many objectives, and many forms. Because no two people are alike, no two people will have exactly the same setup for savings. You have a unique set of needs and objectives for your money, and it is different from everybody else's. There is an account out there to meet every need.

Various savings accounts offer various levels of liquidity. Liquidity refers to whether the money can be accessed instantly or has to be "cashed-out" to access.

Examples of liquid savings include savings accounts, money market accounts, and cash.

Examples of non-liquid savings accounts include 401(k)s, bonds, tangibles and annuities.

Funds in liquid accounts are easy to access via withdrawals, balance transfers, or purchases. Funds in non-liquid savings accounts are locked away by laws and regulations that limit access to funds. Savings in the form of tangible possessions are the least liquid of all savings. Regardless of liquidity, most savings accounts/strategies fit into one of four buckets, depending on the purpose. The four buckets are:

General Savings: Typically used as a buffer for a checking account or short-term expenditures such as down payments, vacations, small unexpected expenses, or just because a little extra accessible money is never a bad thing. General savings are liquid accounts.

Emergency Savings: Often kept away from other bank accounts in an account such as a money market. Ideally, the sum equals 3 to 6 months of living expenses. Emergency savings are always liquid to allow emergency access.

Retirement Savings: These accounts have names like 401(k) and IRA. Retirement accounts are regulated by the federal government and tax code. Anybody can have a retirement account, though the structure is different for employer-sponsored accounts and personal accounts. Generally, funds in these accounts cannot be accessed until the age of 59½. Funds are not liquid.

Health Savings Accounts: This is a new player in the savings market, designed to help people address the rising costs of health care. Health savings accounts may be employer-sponsored or personal. Funds are not taxed and are easily accessible for the purpose of paying qualified healthcare expenses. Funds are not liquid.

Types of Savings Accounts

Savings accounts come in a myriad of forms. Account structure varies considerably depending on purpose and institution. Every type of account is regulated by the federal government, but institutions have some freedom to structure accounts in the way that is most beneficial to them. That is why there are some differences between identical accounts at different institutions.

In order to manage your finances, you need to have a basic understanding of what types of savings accounts are available, how they work, and how they can be most effectively leveraged for your financial situation. The most common types for individuals are savings accounts, retirement accounts, Certificate of Deposit accounts (CDs), annuities, savings bonds, and investments.

Savings Accounts

Checking and savings accounts go together like peanut butter and jelly. Every bank offers standard savings accounts. Most savings accounts pay interest, though interest rates are typically pretty low – among the lowest of any type of savings. Savings accounts improve your credit worthiness and make it easier to get loans – especially when the account is held at the institution from which you are trying to get a loan.

Savings accounts are safer and more secure than keeping cash around the house. Accounts are FDIC insured, which means that deposits up to $250,000 (depending on when the account was created) will be replaced should the bank go out of business, be robbed, or burn to the ground.

Most savings accounts are either free or low-cost but may have minimum balance requirements. This is because banks leverage savings accounts to make loans. Basically, the system works like this:

You deposit your money in the bank. They pay you interest.

They use your funds to make loans, charging interest so that they can make money.

You remain in control of your accounts and can withdraw the funds anytime.

Strategies for Managing Savings Accounts

Set up automatic transfers or deposits. Make it a priority to pay yourself first by building up your savings. Arrange for automatic balance transfers or a portion of your paycheck to be deposited into your savings account.

Set goals. Make a household budget that includes a commitment to build your savings. Calculate how much you can afford to put into savings every month, then make a goal. Use the SMART technique (Specific, Measurable, Achievable, Realistic, Timeline) to set a goal and a reward for achieving the goal. For example: "I will increase my savings by $500 in the next three months. When I hit my goal, I will reward myself with by taking a four-day weekend (or whatever your ideal reward might be)."

Do not touch the savings. Well, perhaps do not touch it is a bit extreme, but you want to be really strategic if you pull from a savings account. It should not be "just because." You worked too hard to spend it for no reason! If you want to pull from your savings account, there should be a specific purpose and a plan to repay. In most cases, it is better to pull from a savings account than to take out a loan when emergencies arise; you do not have to pay interest to borrow from yourself.

Use standard savings as a savings incubator. These accounts are perfect for working toward a goal because the funds remain liquid and they are easy to monitor. Once you reach a milestone, such as the balance you need for an emergency account, move the money to another account and save for another goal.

Choose an account with the highest interest. Interest rates on savings accounts have been remarkably low throughout the first part of the 21st century, so do not expect much. However, shop around for accounts with competitive interest rates. Interest rates usually correspond with minimum balances. High-yield interest savings accounts usually require balances of $10,000 or more.

Certificates of Deposit

Certificate of Deposit (CD) accounts are a type of savings offered by commercial banks and credit unions. They differ from standard savings accounts in that funds are non-liquid for a specific time. The trade-off is that interest rates are double or triple those of standard savings accounts. If an emergency arises, funds in the CD can be accessed, but there are penalties and waiting periods to make withdrawal an unenticing option.

CDs can be short-term or long-term. Long-term CDs pay the highest interest while short-term CDs offer the highest flexibility and liquidity. Typical term lengths for CD accounts include 30 days, 180 days, one year, two years, five years, and ten years. When the term is up, the account holder may cash out the funds or allow the CD to renew. Interest rates vary considerably from institution to institution. In addition, CDs may offer variable interest rates, fixed interest rates, or an option to increase a defined number of times, depending on the market.

Interest may be compounded or deposited to another account. Most people prefer to compound the interest to maximize reward. Compound interest was discussed in Chapter 4. Essentially, the interest is added to the principal, which perpetually increases interest payouts throughout the life of the CD. Interest on Certificate of Deposit accounts is taxed as earned income. If interest paid exceeds a specific amount, the bank will send you a 1099 so you can report it to the IRS.

Strategies for Managing Certificate of Deposit Accounts

Choose the term wisely. As the funds will not be accessible for a specific period of time, make sure you will not need the money. If you are unsure whether the funds will become necessary, opt for a shorter term. This way you will have more frequent opportunities to access the funds should the need arise. Thirty-day terms are excellent for emergency funds or delicate financial situations.

Shop around for high interest rates. Just like standard savings accounts, different financial institutions offer different rates. If your bank does not offer an option that pleases you, shop around. You are not obligated to do all of your banking with one financial institution. CDs are highly regulated, so they operate in much the same way at every institution.

Compound the interest. Most accounts offer the option of depositing interest earned back into the CD or into another account. Depositing the interest into the account increases the principal, which increases the next interest payout. There is nothing better than making your money work harder for you by compounding the interest!

Analyze how interest is paid. This is where institutions vary. Interest payments may be made daily, weekly, monthly, quarterly, annually, or one time. You will make the most money off of daily, weekly, or monthly payments. If you are weighing the options between a higher interest rate and a more frequent payout, break out a calculator to decide which option is best.

Annuities

This type of account is typically used as a part of a trust fund or a retirement portfolio. In essence, an annuity is an account that makes payments to you. You make a deposit and receive payments for the rest of your life. Most annuities are operated through insurance companies, not financial institutions – though most major commercial banks also sell insurance.

Annuities may be deferred or immediate. Deferred annuities are built up over time and payments start at a certain age or after a defined period of time. Immediate annuities result in immediate payouts and are typically used to stabilize retirement income. Funds deposited to annuities earn money in one of three ways:

1. Funds are used to invest in CDs, loans, or bonds. These are known as Fixed Annuities. Interest rates and payouts are guaranteed. There is little risk, but the payouts are lower in relation to the deposit.

2. Funds are invested in market indices such as the S&P 500. These are known as Indexed Annuities. Most of these accounts include protection against loss and earnings caps. This type of annuity is considered balanced because it minimizes risk to the owner and the payouts tend to be higher than with fixed annuities.

3. Funds are invested in stocks, commodities, and other equity instruments. These annuities are known as Variable Annuities. Interest rates and payouts are not guaranteed because they are tied to the market. There is more risk, but payouts are usually the highest of the three structures.

The biggest advantage of annuities is that they produce income but cannot be outlived. The insurance company essentially manages the money and makes payments to you in accordance with the terms of the account your entire life. Though most people consider annuities a retirement strategy, anybody can use an annuity to stabilize income.

Payments from annuities are typically taxed as normal income, which can be a drawback for some people. In addition, the institution may charge fees for administration. If you need the money, there may be withdrawal penalties. The other disadvantage to an annuity is that the return on investment may be lower than it is with other types of accounts. These are trade-offs for the extraordinary benefits of lifetime income and wealth protection.

Savings Bonds

The federal government offers a type of savings known as a savings bond. Savings bonds are a simple and straightforward way to save and grow your money. They tend to be incredibly stable, and returns are predictable. Savings bonds are intended for long-term savings. Terms and interest rates are declared by the United States Treasury because savings bonds are sold to raise funds for the government.

There are two types of savings bonds: EE/E and I. EE/E Savings Bonds are purchased at face value and earn interest for up to 30 years. The interest rate for the first 20 years is fixed. I Savings Bonds are also purchased at face value and also earn interest for up to 30 years. I Savings Bonds combine a fixed rate and an inflation rate intended to protect the bond against inflation.

If the bond is cashed in before it is five years old, the account holder will lose the prior three months' interest. Interest is taxable at regular income rates unless the income is used to pay for an education.

An interesting feature of savings bonds is that they can be given as a gift. They are a popular way for people to give money to children because of the education benefit. Savings bonds can also be used to stabilize a portfolio and earn guaranteed income.

EE/E Bonds are easy to predict because interest rates are guaranteed, but inflation can mitigate earned interest. I Bonds tend to be more lucrative, but earnings are less predictable. Interest rates vary and may be as low as 0%.

Neither option offers exceptional returns, but they also carry exceptionally low risk. They are a good way to lock money away to keep it out of sight and out of mind. For people who have a hard time keeping their hands off their money, savings bonds can be just what the doctor ordered.

Retirement Accounts

Most retirement accounts are heavily regulated investment accounts, not cash-based savings accounts. The concept is to protect and grow money until you are old enough to retire. Retirement accounts also benefit financial institutions because the funds are not liquid, so the institution can use the funds to make investments of their own. With most retirement accounts, you must be at least 59½ years old to begin taking withdrawals; otherwise you will pay a penalty and tax.

Every retirement account is an investment account. You dictate where funds are invested within the options provided by the account. Typical options include mutual funds, stocks, and bonds. The performance of your account is based on how well your investments perform.

Each structure offers specific tax benefits. The money is taxed either when it is deposited or when it is withdrawn. We will cover the pros and cons of various retirement plan accounts a little bit later.

Investments

Investments include direct purchases of stocks, bonds, ETFs, mutual funds, and a variety of other investments. They tend to be the highest-risk way of managing savings. In many ways, investments are like gambling. You may lose every dime, or you could win big and make gigantic returns. The results of investments are unpredictable and tied to the economy.

If you want to make investments, you must be willing to lose every dime that you invest. In other words, investments should not be your primary long-term savings strategy. Investments are best relegated to playing a role in retirement planning as an option to generate income without working.

The old saying is that it "takes money to make money," and that is 100% true with investments. You will have to pay brokerage fees to process transactions and maintain your account. There are also tax implications.

Investments are purchased with post-tax dollars.

When you sell and make a profit, you have to pay capital gains tax.

Capital gains taxes are typically a flat percentage, like 20%. On the flipside, if you lose money in the market, you can also deduct that from your taxable income.

Investments are risky and are not for everybody. Though you can enter the market with any amount of money, typically you need at least $1,000 in order to cover trading fees and taxes. Some investments offer tax benefits while others are questionable and possibly even illegal. Before jumping into investing, you need to do a lot of research to decide on a strategy. It is always a good idea to consult with certified experts before investing a dime.

Savings and You

Ultimately, how you choose to save your money is up to you. There is no right or wrong answer – it is all determined by your financial situation, your objectives, and your goals. Do not feel like you have to do one thing or another – because your money is in your control. Most people use a combination of accounts and strategies. Typically, people try to spread out risk between investments and liquid savings so that they do not lose everything if the market turns south.

The most common roadmap for savings is:

Build emergency savings equal to 3-6 months of total expenses. Sock it away, but keep it liquid.

Begin amassing retirement savings and develop your personal retirement strategy.

Goal-oriented savings happens at the same time as retirement savings.

Stabilize income with investments – this may happen at any time.

Stabilize retirement income – this typically happens right before and during retirement.

Because savings has an impact on taxes, it is a good idea to consult with a tax professional before jumping into anything that can a tie up your money for an extended period of time. To schedule a time to discuss your best savings options, please give my office a call at (207) 741-2400.

Retirement

Personal finance management should never be driven by fear; it is a matter of logic and math. However, if not planned for, retirement can generate copious amounts of fear. There is no shortage of compelling reasons why you should be planning for your retirement. The biggest is that as we age, our bodies and minds do not operate as well as they do when we are young. This is not to say that everybody who is elderly is incapable of being a productive, income-earning contributor to the economy. It's just that working becomes more taxing on body, mind, and soul.

Though the United States provides retirement benefits to senior citizens, it is rarely enough to make ends meet. The average Social Security benefit for retired couples in January 2013 was $2,014 per month. For many people, that is barely enough to cover the mortgage/rent. Though the system does fulfill its purpose of assisting retired folks, it fails to provide enough for them to be fully independent.

Despite the political rhetoric around Social Security, the system is self-sustaining and can continue to be indefinitely, provided Congress does its job. No matter what the future of Social Security might be, you can count on the fact that you will need to pay for at least a portion of your own retirement.

For most people, retirement is an objective, a goal, and a rare time in life where you can do what you want to do. Counting on Social Security or your family is not a good way to meet that objective. Retirement is much more enjoyable when you have enough money to live comfortably, and a little left over to spend. You can't enjoy it as much if you are a burden to your family or have to rely on piddly government checks that barely cover the bills.

Successful retirement planning works with a variety of income sources such as Social Security, 401(k), pensions, investments, and other savings strategies. In most cases, it takes multiple sources of income to create a comfortable level of financial security. You do not have to be rich to retire well; you just have to be smart and prepared. Nobody is going to give you a free ride when you retire; your retirement is entirely your responsibility.

Social Security

Social Security is a program created by President Franklin Delano Roosevelt in 1935. It was enacted as a response to the fact that over 50% of the nation's senior citizens were living in poverty. Since enacted, the program has evolved to cover every worker, including the self-employed. The program also offers disability insurance and survivorship benefits under certain circumstances.

The program is funded by a few different income taxes. Receipts are deposited into the Social Security Trust Fund, which is managed by the United States Treasury. Essentially, today's workers are cutting today's Social Security checks. When revenues exceed expenditures, the surplus is invested into government bonds for safekeeping. When expenditures exceed revenues, the bonds are cashed.

Much of the political rhetoric around Social Security involves the way those bonds are issued. As it stands, they contribute to the Federal Government's budget deficit – so that's why all the noise. It is a bit of an unusual system and is the subject of much debate, criticism, or praise – depending on who is talking.

The bottom line is that Social Security plays a vital role in retirement planning because it is income you can count on. No matter how young or old you are, you have Social Security benefits waiting in the wings. The actual benefit will depend on what you earn over your working life. The more you earn, the larger your benefit will be.

Strategies for Preparing for Social Security

As you approach retirement, starting at 10-15 years out, keep an eye on your estimated Social Security benefits. The Social Security Administration makes it quite simple, because it provides annual benefit estimates. Set up an online account at ssa.gov/myaccount or visit a local Social Security office to receive an estimate.

Once you know what your benefits will be, work with other components of your retirement strategy to round out and stabilize forecasted income. Common action steps include increasing contributions to retirement accounts, juggling investments, etc.

Forecast your taxes. (All financial calculations need to include taxes.) You may be required to pay taxes on your Social Security benefits. In the worst-case scenario, up to 85% of your benefits might be taxed. There are many conditions and factors that influence your tax rates. Consult with a tax professional to understand tax implications for your benefits. The last thing you want is to be surprised with a whopping tax bill just as you are entering your golden years!

Pensions

In the United States, pensions are typically administered by the government, labor unions, and a few employers. Pensions are funded by contributions from employer and employee, with benefits paid to the employee after retirement. Many pension programs also include some insurance-like aspects such as paying survivorship or disability benefits. Pensions and Social Security operate in much the same way.

Pensions are different from most retirement plans like IRAs or 401(k), because they are usually not tied to market returns. Pension payments tend to be paid out like a fixed annuity in that the beneficiary receives payments for an unlimited period of time after retirement. Payments usually do not change. Plans like these are also known as Defined Benefit Pension Plans. There are two classifications for funding – the plan is either "unfunded" or "funded."

Unfunded pensions are often administered by governments. Benefits are paid on the PAYGO (pay-as-you-go) structure, which means that funding comes from current workers' contributions to the pension program.

Funded pensions collect contributions from the employer and employees and use the money to make investments. Benefits are paid out of the fund. Typically, the employer assumes the risk for the investments, though there are some pensions that vary benefits based on fund performance.

If you are fortunate enough to have a pension plan, your payout is usually calculated based upon:

1. How long you worked
2. How much you made
3. Your age
4. Various other factors

Every organization has a different way of calculating and managing benefits. Some include adjustments for inflation, some do not. Also, some benefits may be payable upon termination of the job if you quit or get fired before you retire. It just depends on the way the plan is set up and how your employment contract is worded.

In the United States, private employers (except for churches) are required to guarantee their pensions by purchasing insurance from the Pension Benefit Guarantee Corporation. Insurance, plenty of regulation, and employer-assumed risk make pensions a desirable part of a retirement package.

Unfortunately, most employers have scratched pensions and only offer IRAs or 401(k). A couple of generations ago, pretty much everybody that worked for a big company got a pension. Employers decided they no longer wanted to bear the risk, cost, and responsibility of a traditional pension and have adopted other ways to help employees retire – though many offer nothing. Government, executive management, and military jobs are some of the few that still provide pensions.

Investments

Investments are a big, complex world, and this section is just going to touch on some of the popular ways that people use investments to fund retirement. When it comes to investing for retirement, there are a multitude of approaches. The most traditional approach is to open a brokerage account and trade stocks, bonds, and mutual funds. Investments can also take on other forms such as real estate, business ventures, peer-to-peer lending, precious metals and other valuable materials, working interest shares in oil wells, etc.

Investments can be quite creative. Some of the most creative and lucrative investments are made behind closed doors between personal parties. For example, grandparents may lend grandchildren money to go to college in exchange for regular payments in the future. Another creative example would be making a loan (under contract) to a family member to start a business in exchange for a share of the profits. Creative investments tend to be risky, but also rewarding. If you are interested in doing creative investments, do yourself a favor and make sure you have a solid contract in place before you hand over a single dollar! As with any investing, you need to be willing to part with the money, as it may not come back. Risk is much higher with creative investments.

If you are planning on using investments to help fund your retirement, you need to understand that the risk of losing your money is higher than it is with retirement accounts. Because retirement accounts are set up by investment firms that have a stake in the success of the account, there is inherently less risk. When you are investing on your own, you are more likely to make mistakes and lose your money. However, you can also do quite well for yourself. You must understand your risk tolerance. It is a good idea to work with a highly qualified professional that has your best interests at heart.

In the next chapter, we'll explore the most common vehicles for personal retirement savings: Retirement accounts.

Retirement Tax Planning: Are You In The Right Retirement Plan?

Special types of investment accounts that are intended purely for retirement savings come with a wide range of ta x benefits. These special types of accounts are the primary means by which most Americans save for their retirement.

When it comes to choosing your retirement plan, you need to decide which plan gives you the best combination of contribution benefits, flexibility, and liquidity.

I'm not here to make you an expert on retirement plans. But I can help you decide pretty quickly if the plan you have is right for you – or if you should be looking for something more suited for your specific needs. So bear with me, even if the next few pages look intimidating. These are some very powerful strategies.

We'll assume for the purposes of this discussion that you've already decided you want to save more than the $5,500 you can save in an IRA. We'll also assume, at least for the next few pages, that you want a "traditional" arrangement, where you deduct the contributions you make now and pay tax on withdrawals. (We'll address alternatives, including Roth arrangements and life insurance, towards the end of the chapter.)

SEP

The Simplified Employee Pension, or "SEP," is the easiest plan to set up because it's just a turbocharged IRA:

If you're self-employed, you can contribute and deduct up to 25% of your "net self-employment income."

If your business is incorporated and you're salaried, you can contribute 25% of your "covered compensation," which essentially means your salary.

The maximum contribution for any single employee 2015 is $53,000.

If you've got employees, you'll have to contribute for them, too. You generally have to contribute the same percentage for your employees as you do for yourself. However, if your income is significantly higher than that of your employees, you can use what's called an "integrated" formula to make extra contributions for higher incomes.

The money goes straight into regular IRA accounts you set up for yourself and your employees. There's no annual administration or paperwork required.

SEP assets accumulate tax-deferred over time. You'll pay tax at ordinary income rates when you withdraw them in retirement. There are penalties for early withdrawals before age 59½, and for failing to take required minimum distributions beginning at age 70½.

The SEP is easy to adopt, easy to maintain, and flexible. If there's no money to contribute, you just don't contribute. But remember, the contribution is limited to a percentage of your covered compensation. So, for example, if you set up an S corporation to limit your self-employment tax, you'll also limit your SEP contribution because it's based on that lower salary amount.

SIMPLE

The next step up the retirement plan ladder is the SIMPLE IRA. This is another "turbocharged" IRA that lets you contribute more than the usual $5,500 limit:

You and your employees can "defer" and deduct 100% of your income up to $12,500. If your income is under $50,000, that may be more than you could sock away with a SEP.

If you're 50 or older you can make an extra $3,000 "catch up" contribution.

But – you have to match everyone's deferral or make profit-sharing contributions. You can match employee contributions dollar-for-dollar up to 3% of their pay, or contribute 2% of everyone's pay whether they choose to defer or not. If you choose the match, you can reduce it as low as 1% for two years out of five.

The money goes straight into employee IRAs. You can designate a single financial institution to hold the money, or let your employees choose where to hold their accounts.

There's no set-up charge or annual administration fee.

SIMPLE assets accumulate tax-deferred over time. You'll pay tax at ordinary income rates when you withdraw them in retirement. There are penalties for early withdrawals before age 59½, and failing to take required minimum distributions beginning at age 70½.

The SIMPLE IRA may be best for part-time or sideline businesses earning less than $50,000, because the flat $12,500 contribution is higher than the 25% SEP contribution for incomes up to $50,000.

401(k)

The next step up the retirement plan ladder is the 401(k), and this is the type of plan you most likely have access to if you are an employee at a large company. Most people think of 401(k)s as retirement plans for bigger businesses, but you can set up a 401(k) for any size business. In fact, you can even set up what's called a "solo" or "individual" 401(k) just for yourself.

The 401(k) is a true "qualified" plan. This means you'll set up a trust, adopt a written plan agreement, and choose a trustee. But the 401(k) lets you contribute far more money, far more flexibly, than either the SEP or the SIMPLE.

You and your employees can "defer" and deduct 100% of your income up to $18,000. If you're 50 or older, you can make an extra $6,000 "catch up" contribution.

You can choose to match contributions, or make "profit-sharing" contributions up to 25% of everyone's pay. (If you operate as an S corporation, you can contribute up to 25% of your salary, but not any pass-through distributions.) That's the same percentage you can save in your SEP – on top of the $18,000 deferral.

The maximum contribution for 2015 is $53,000 per person, plus any "catch up" contributions.

You can offer yourself and your employees loans, hardship withdrawals, and all the bells and whistles "the big boys" offer their employees. If you're an employee, make sure that you are at least contributing the minimum amount to max out your employer matching contribution.

You can use "cross-testing" to skew profit-sharing contributions to favored employees. "Age weighted" plans allocate more to older employees (on the theory that they have less time to save for retirement); "integrated" and "super-integrated" plans allocate more to higher-paid employees (on the theory that they get no benefit from Social Security for their income above the Social Security wage base); and "rate group" plans divide employees into groups (such as managers, administrators, and salespeople) and make different contributions for each group.

401(k) assets accumulate tax-deferred over time. You'll pay tax at ordinary income rates when you withdraw them in retirement. There are penalties for early withdrawals before age 59½, and failing to take required minimum distributions beginning at age 70½.

The downside? 401(k)s are true "qualified" plans, which makes them harder to administer than SEPs or SIMPLEs. You have to establish a qualified-plan trust to hold plan assets. The trust will have to file Form 5500, an informational return reporting contributions and assets, every year. And there are complicated anti-discrimination and "top-heavy" rules to keep you from stuffing your own account while you stiff your employees.

However, if the 401(k) really does make sense, there are three alternatives that might make administration easier:

A "SIMPLE" 401(k) avoids nondiscrimination and top-heavy rules in exchange for guaranteed employer contributions. You and your employees can defer 25% of covered compensation up to the SIMPLE plan contribution limits. Your business has to contribute 2% of covered comp or match contributions up to 3% of covered comp. This works if you want a true 401(k), but you're afraid your employees won't contribute enough to let you make meaningful deferrals. You can also convert an existing 401(k) to a SIMPLE 401(k).

A "Safe Harbor" 401(k) avoids nondiscrimination (but not top-heavy) rules in exchange for bigger employee contributions. You and your employees can defer up to the regular 401(k) limit. You can either: 1) contribute 3% of covered comp; or 2) match contributions dollar-for-dollar up to 3% of covered comp and fifty-cents-on-the-dollar for contributions between 3% and 5% of covered comp. You can even make extra profit sharing contributions on top of the required contributions.

If you operate a business all by yourself, with no employees other than your spouse, you can establish an "individual" 401(k) with less red tape.

Defined Benefit Plans

Finally, if you want to contribute more than the $53,000 limit for SEPs or 401(k)s, you might consider a defined benefit plan. This is your father's retirement plan – the traditional "pension plan" that so many employers have stopped offering because they can't afford it anymore. However, it can still be a great choice for older, highly compensated business owners with few employees.

Defined benefit plans let you guarantee up to $210,000 in annual income (2105 limit).

You can contribute – and deduct – as much as you need to finance that benefit. You'll calculate those contributions according to your age, your desired retirement age, your current income, and various actuarial factors.

A 412(i) plan (sometimes called a 412(e) plan), which is funded entirely with life insurance or annuities, lets you contribute even more.

The biggest problem with the defined benefit plan is the required annual contributions. If your business doesn't have the money, you still have to pay. However, you can combine a defined benefit plan with a 401(k) or SEP to give yourself a little more flexibility. Let's say you could contribute up to $100,000 to a defined benefit plan, but you're not confident you can commit to that much every year. You might set up a defined benefit plan with a $50,000 contribution, then pair it with 401(k) for another $50,000. If business is poor in a particular year, you can choose to skip the 401(k) that year.

Roth's World

So, now that we've covered the menu of traditional employer-sponsored retirement plans, let's throw another wrench into the mix. Do you even want or need a traditional plan? Or would you be better off with an alternative? Perhaps even giving up the current tax break?

All of the plans we've discussed so far assume that you're better off taking a tax deduction for plan contributions now, as they go in the plan, then letting plan assets accumulate tax-free over time, and then paying tax on withdrawals, at ordinary income rates, when you need them for retirement.

That's a great strategy if your tax rate is higher now than it will be in retirement. You benefit now by avoiding tax on contributions, which puts more to work for you today. And you benefit later by paying less tax on withdrawals.

But that traditional pattern doesn't always hold true. Maybe you're young, just starting your career, and your income is low. Maybe you're transitioning from one career or business to another, and your income is temporarily low. Maybe you think that tax rates in general will rise. (Today's top marginal rate may seem high at 39.6%, but that's actually quite low by historical standards.) Sometimes, contributing to a traditional retirement plan creates a ticking tax time bomb and actually costs you money over the long run.

Here are two alternatives you might consider if standard qualified plans don't fit the bill:

"Roth" accounts take the traditional defer-now, pay-later arrangement and turn it on its head. The basic Roth IRA doesn't give you any deduction for contributions you make today. But your withdrawals are generally tax-free so long as they've "aged" at least five years. Tax-free income sounds great, right? However, contributions are limited to $5,500 per year ($6,500 if you're 50 or older), and you can't contribute at all if your income is over $131,000 (single filers) or $193,000 (joint filers). (If your income is above those limits, you can still fund a Roth by contributing the maximum to a nondeductible traditional IRA, then immediately convert it to a Roth.)

If you sponsor a 401(k), you can choose to designate your salary deferrals up to $18,000 as "Roth" deferrals. You won't get any deduction today, but your withdrawals down the road will be tax-free. (Any employer contributions will continue to be treated as deductible now and taxable later.)

If you have a SEP, you can create a backdoor "Roth SEP" by making a regular deductible SEP contribution, then immediately converting it to a Roth. Roth conversions in general are a subject for another book – I just want you to be aware that the possibility exists.

Sean T. O'Hare, CPA

Life Insurance

Life insurance policies as a retirement planning vehicle? You bet!

Permanent life insurance policies that include a cash value can offer several significant tax breaks for supplemental retirement savings. There's no deduction for premiums you pay into the contract. But policy cash values grow tax-deferred. And you can take cash from your policy, tax-free, by withdrawing your original premiums and then borrowing against remaining cash values. You'll pay (nondeductible) interest on your loan, but earn it back on your cash value. Many insurers offer "wash loan" provisions that let you borrow against your policy with little or no out-of-pocket costs.

.These advantages aren't completely unlimited. If you stuff too much cash into the policy in the first seven years, it's considered a "modified endowment contract" and all withdrawals are taxed as ordinary income until you exhaust your inside buildup.

Insurers offer three main types of cash-value policies with three different investment profiles to suit different investors. The key is finding a policy that matches your investment temperament.

"Whole life" resembles a bank CD in a tax-advantaged wrapper, with required annual premiums and strong guarantees. Remember when we said the defined benefit pension was your father's pension plan? Well, this is your father's life insurance.

"Universal life" resembles a bond fund in a tax-advantaged wrapper, with flexible premiums but less strong guarantees.

"Variable life" lets you invest cash values in a series of "subaccounts" resembling mutual funds in a tax-deferred wrapper. You can choose "variable whole life" with required premiums and stronger guarantees, or "variable universal life" contracts with flexible premiums and less strong guarantees.

Once again, I'm not here to make you an expert in retirement plans or alternatives. My goal is simply to open your eyes to the wide variety of plans and options so that you can evaluate if the plan you have now is really the right plan for you.

For a comprehensive and personalized review of your retirement plan options, feel free to call my office at (207) 741-2400 to schedule a consultation.

Your Home As A Retirement Asset

The primary residence is often a substantial chunk of a person's net worth, but it often ignored as a retirement asset. Because most people purchase a home in their 30s, chances are good that the home will be paid off by retirement. Some people choose to stay in the home, and other people choose to sell it. There are advantages and disadvantages to each.

Staying in the Home. If you choose to live in a home you own outright, you will only be responsible for property taxes and insurance. Property continues to be an asset and can be borrowed against in the future. It can also generate income if you decide to rent out a portion of the house or take out a reverse mortgage. The disadvantage is that the property taxes may be more than you can afford, and the home may just be impractical or unnecessary – a lot of retirees complain about their family homes being "too big" or having "too many stairs."

Selling the home. If you choose to sell the home, you can use that money to invest, purchase an annuity, purchase a more appropriate home, move somewhere you have always wanted to move, move in with family and use the money to sustain yourself, etc. The disadvantage is that you lose out on the value of the home as an asset as well as future increases in property value.

The goal of any retirement plan should be to support yourself as you live out your days. For most people, it takes multiple income sources. Social Security is a major part, but insufficient for most people.

Retirement is serious business. Even if you have family and support, you should not count on them to support you in your retirement. It is not fair to them or you! You do not know what they will be doing when you retire, and it is not fair to expect them to take care of you. In addition, retirement is a wonderful time of life, for you are no longer required to work every day – why would you want to diminish that by being beholden to another?

Part IV: Taxing It

Sean T. O'Hare, CPA

Personal Taxes

It takes a peculiar person to enjoy doing taxes. If you are like most people, you deplore doing your taxes. It is no wonder too, with the U.S. tax code being as complicated as it is. The tax code is so big and so complex that people cannot even agree on how big it is. Some people say it is the equivalent of seven Bibles. Others say that it is over 1 million pages long. Whatever it truly is, it is a massive, complicated mess of print on paper. Fortunately, only a small portion of the code applies to typical personal taxes.

This chapter is going to take a closer look at personal taxes. Along the way, strategies will be highlighted that are intended to help you manage and prepare for filing your taxes. While there will be a lot of good information, it is certainly no substitute for a qualified tax professional. Please use this information as a reference, and if you have additional questions, reach out to a qualified accountant who can help you understand your responsibility.

Also note that the majority the material is specific to filing federal taxes; however, most state taxes are remarkably similar to federal taxes. You can pretty much assume that the terms, responsibilities, and methods are the same. Keep in mind that you are liable for paying federal, state, and municipal taxes. If you make estimated tax payments, remember to include estimated taxes to the state and applicable municipalities in your calculations.

Why Do We Pay Taxes?

A lot of people get bent out of shape over taxes. It is understandable, because you work hard for your money and it does not seem fair to hand it over to somebody who does not even have the courtesy to give you a receipt. However, taxes are a vital part of the economy and one of the reasons that people living in the U.S. experience some the highest standards of living mankind has ever known. There is also an interesting history to explain how we ended up with our current tax code.

It is a bit ironic that the U.S. has such a complicated tax code, because the reason the Colonies rebelled against the British was taxes. After the United States won its independence from Britain, the Founding Fathers went to work creating a new government. The Second Continental Congress convened in June of 1776. As the country had declared its independence, it now needed a government of some type to manage the affairs. The meeting had some interesting results and set an anti-tax precedent.

The Articles of Confederation created a weak central government that had no ability to tax. It was not until the Constitution was ratified that the federal government had the ability to levy and collect taxes. It took all the way until 1861 for the United States to ratify an income tax. It was intended, in part, to fund the Civil War and was repealed in 1872. There were some legal struggles over income tax between 1872 and 1913 until the 16th amendment was ratified. The clause declares:

"The Congress shall have power to lay and collect taxes on incomes, from whatever source derived, without apportionment among the several States, and without regard to any census or enumeration."

A broad sweeping income tax was passed in 1913, and the country has never looked back. During World War II, quarterly tax payments and payroll withholding were introduced and became the basis for our extensive (and expensive) tax code. Over the years, payroll taxes have undergone many ups and downs, and layers and layers of revisions, to bring us to the point where we are today. Every year, Congress adds to the tax code to fund various programs and projects in response to lobbying and to appeal to their constituency. Now it should be clear why we have such an extensive, confusing code.

With such a beast of a tax code to adhere to, it's easy to fall into numerous pitfalls when it comes to complying with the tax laws. Over the next few pages, we'll examine some of the most common mistakes that people make in regards to their taxes.

Failing To Plan

I don't care how good you and your tax preparer are with a stack of receipts on April 15. If you didn't know you could write off your kid's braces as a business expense, there's nothing we can do.

Remember the last time you drove a car? If you're like most people, you probably sat down in the driver's seat, strapped on your seat belt, turned the ignition, put the car in reverse, then backed your way to your destination, steering by what you could see out the rear view mirror.

Wait a minute... You mean that's not how you do it?

Well, that's how most tax preparers work. They spend lots of time looking back at what you did last year. But they don't spend much time looking forward. They can tell you all about what you did yesterday. But they don't tell you what you should do today, or when you should do it or how you should do it.

Tax planning, on the other hand, provides two powerful benefits you can't get anywhere else.

First, it's the key to your financial defense. Generally, you have two ways to put cash in your pocket. There's financial offense, which means making more. And there's financial defense, which means spending less. For most of you reading this book, spending less is easier than making more.

And for most of you reading this book, <u>taxes are your single biggest expense</u>. So it makes sense to focus your financial defense where you spend the most. Sure, you can save 15% on car insurance by switching to GEICO. But how much will that really save in the long run?

Second, tax planning guarantees results. You can spend all sorts of time, effort, and money promoting your business or completing more education in an effort to get a raise – and that still won't guarantee results. Or you can set up a medical expense reimbursement plan, deduct the cost of your teenage daughter's braces, and guarantee savings.

Those guaranteed results start with planning. You can't ever deduct money you spend on a medical expense reimbursement plan if you don't set it up in the first place.

Now that we understand why planning is so important, let's take a quick look at how the tax system works. This will "lay a foundation" for understanding the specific strategies we'll be talking about soon.

Income Taxes

Income taxes are the taxes you pay on the money you earn. Before we dive into it, let's take a look at some of the common terms associated with income taxes. It is important to understand these terms and what they mean because they help to decode the tax code.

Gross income: The IRS defines gross income as the sum of all money, goods, property, and services not exempted from taxes. Gross income includes wages, salary, contract earnings, winnings, capital gains, social security, interest, certain debts that have been written off, and the value of any goods you exchanged for services – yes, even barter is taxed.

Filing Status: Determines how your taxes are calculated. It is based on your marital and family status.

Single means that you are unmarried, divorced, or legally separated.

Married Filing Jointly means that you and your spouse are filing a return as one. This is one of the most beneficial statuses.

Married Filing Separately is for couples that are married but are filing their taxes separately for various reasons. The IRS penalizes this group by offering smaller deductions, exemptions, and credits.

Head of Household is for unmarried taxpayers that have children or care for a qualifying person. The calculations are almost as favorable as Married Filing Jointly.

Qualifying Widower with Dependent Child is the status for people who have lost their spouse and are still caring for their children. This status is very limited in regards to who can use it.

Deductions: These are subtractions from your taxable income. Deductions are considered before tax is calculated. They reduce your tax bill by reducing the amount of money you are required to pay taxes on.

Credits: These are subtractions from your tax bill. Credits are applied after deductions and taxes are calculated. They may reduce or eliminate your tax liability. Certain credits may result in a refund.

Exemptions: Every taxpayer is entitled to an exemption. It essentially exempts a certain amount of your income from taxes.

Understanding Tax Calculation

The IRS does not make it easy to understand how to calculate taxes. Different types of income are taxed at different rates, each filing status is entitled to different credits/deductions, and just to keep you on your toes, Congress changes tax rates, credits, deductions, and exemptions every year.

Deductions

Deductions are an interesting part of the tax code. As mentioned before, deductions reduce the amount of income on which you will pay taxes. So if you made $50,000 last year, and your deductions total up to $20,000, then you only have to pay taxes on $30,000. There are literally thousands of deductions available, but few people can use them all. Each tends to be focused on specific groups and specific situations. However, every taxpayer does use deductions when calculating taxes.

Every taxpayer is entitled to the standard deduction, and most people have a handful of other deductions they are entitled to claim. It is also vital to understand the difference between itemized deductions, the standard deduction, and other deductions to determine taxable income.

Standard Deduction: The government figures that every person has a certain amount of income that is not eligible for taxes because it was spent on non-reimbursed employee expenses, medical bills, and various other expenses. Essentially, the government gives you a free pass on a portion of your income. The standard deduction is a flat rate and is based on your filing status.

Itemized Deductions: When you have more deductions than the standard deduction, you can claim itemized deductions. Common itemized deductions include interest on your mortgage, medical bills, charitable donations, and casualty/theft losses. There are many other types of expenses that can be added into itemized deductions as well.

Other Deductions: Most other deductions are factored in when calculating AGI (adjusted gross income). These include things such as educator expenses, contributions to qualified retirement plans, student loan interest, health savings accounts deductions, and much more.

There is a sticking point with deductions. Unless it is the standard deduction, you need to have documentation to prove that you are eligible for the deduction if you are audited. For most of these deductions, it is pretty straightforward because you receive bills and statements to prove the expense. For deductions like educator expenses, non-reimbursed employee expenses, or charitable donations, you must have receipts, logs, and other valid documentation to show the IRS if they have questions.

Credits

Credits are the fun part of tax calculation. Every credit you apply reduces the dollars you have to pay to the government. Some credits are "refundable" which means that the government may end up paying you money after refunding all of your paid taxes. For the most part, credits are straightforward. Common credits are childcare expenses, education credits, credits for contributions to retirement accounts, tax credits for having children, and more.

The EITC (Earned Income Tax Credit) is one of the most notable tax credits. It benefits individuals and families with low to moderate income and was created to encourage people to work instead of depending on payments from social programs such as welfare. It is a refundable tax credit, which means that if you are eligible, you may end up receiving free money from the government. The tax credit is most beneficial to married couples with children who earn under $50,000 a year. The more children you have, the bigger the credit.

Credits are straightforward because they are black and white. Either you are eligible for them or you are not. If you are not sure whether you are eligible for a certain tax credit, you need to read through the IRS's instructions carefully. If you are still unsure (which is common) then you need to consult a tax professional. Sometimes the language used to write the tax code is unintelligible and confusing, so there is no shame in not understanding it!

Paying Income Tax

When it comes actually paying your taxes, the IRS has actually made it pretty painless and convenient. Taxes are either withheld, paid quarterly, or paid every year. They can be paid through check, money order, or by authorizing a payment directly from your bank account.

Withholding

If you are an employee, then taxes are deducted from your paycheck. The company handles calculation and processing. Your employer holds your tax deductions in trust and pays them to the IRS every quarter. You fill out a W-9 form and they use that information to calculate your deductions. Relatively little work is required from you until it is time to file taxes.

Though it may be frustrating to see all that money taken out of your check every week, just remember that it is very convenient. If that money was not taken out your check every week, you would be required to make quarterly estimated tax payments. That would mean that you would have to calculate what you owe and cut a check to the IRS every quarter. Being an employee also means that you are excused from penalties associated with underpaying estimated taxes.

Estimated Taxes

If you are self-employed, a business owner, or make money from gambling winnings, lottery winnings, etc., you probably have to pay estimated taxes. Anybody who is not subject to payroll withholding is likely responsible for paying estimated taxes. They are due January 15th, April 15th, July 15th, and September 15th. The government gives you a pass in December so that you can go Christmas shopping.

Estimated taxes are challenging because there is no defined way to calculate them. Also, the IRS does not send you a receipt for the estimated taxes you paid; you have to keep track of that for yourself. The general rule of thumb with estimated taxes is that you should be paying at least the same amount in taxes as you did the prior year. If your income goes up, you need to adjust your estimated tax payment up; if your income goes down you may adjust them down – but you may pique the interest of the IRS.

Be aware that underpaying estimated taxes may result in penalties and interest. This is only if you owe more than $1,000 when you file your taxes on April 15. If you are close, the penalties and interest will be minimal. If not, it can be an expensive and stressful mistake. You do not want to be the taxpayer that files his or her taxes only to realize that you grossly underestimated your payments.

On the flipside, if you overpay estimated taxes, you can get a refund or opt to have those estimated taxes applied to the next year. If anything, you want to pay more in estimated taxes than you owe to avoid problems.

Properly calculating your Estimated Tax Payments is important in order to avoid penalties. For assistance, give me a call at (207) 741-2400.

One thing you may need to decide is whether you prefer convenience or the opportunity to earn interest. If one spouse is employed, you may increase withholding to avoid making quarterly payments to the IRS. You may still need to make payments to your state or municipality. Simply file a revised W-9 form and ask the company to increase withholding by a specific dollar amount every paycheck. This dollar amount needs to add up to your estimated tax payment.

The advantage of paycheck withholding is that it eliminates the need to cut checks every quarter. For a lot of people, this is preferred because it is simpler.

The advantage of paying quarterly is that you can earn a little interest on the money. Every time you make money, withhold it for yourself. Deposit the withholding in short-term CDs or high interest savings accounts. This way you can earn a few extra bucks on your money before it is handed over to the government. Make sure you make the payments on time!

AMT (Alternative Minimum Tax)

Alternative Minimum Tax is a tax on the books designed to ensure that wealthy individuals and businesses are paying at least a minimum amount of taxes. It is a flat rate based on taxable income above a specific level. It is one of the most complex and confusing income taxes and applies to few situations.

For a very limited number of taxpayers, AMT is a trap that results in extraordinary tax liability. In order to address this, Congress frequently changes income thresholds and applies patches. Until 2012, with the passage of the American Taxpayer Relief Act of 2012, there was no clause in the code that adjusted income levels for inflation. It resulted in disaster for some households. Even with the adjustments put into place in 2012, the AMT still captures some households that it actually should not.

Unless you make a lot of money from dividends, or make over $78,000 per year (married filing jointly), you probably do not have to worry about AMT. Because AMT is complex and there are lots of loopholes and exceptions, consult with a tax professional to determine if and how much you may owe.

Taxes on Retirement Income

Trying to grasp taxes on retirement income is enough to make the most intelligent people scratch their heads in wonder. This is because the taxability of your retirement income varies based on whether you are still working, whether your spouse is still working, how much you make, your filing status, and whether or not your distributions are taxable.

Unless you are collecting distributions from a Roth IRA or specific type of tax-sheltered annuity, you can expect to pay taxes on at least a portion of the income you receive. For example, with Social Security the IRS declares a base amount as the threshold for determining when taxes are due. If ½ of your Social Security + all other income = more than the base amount, Social Security benefits are taxable.

One thing you can count on with retirement income taxes is that your tax liability will be different than it was when you were working. For most people, it goes down – but that depends on how you are making money. If you are in retirement or nearing retirement, the best idea is to consult a tax professional to understand your new tax situation.

Other Taxes to Keep on the Radar

Certain situations may result in additional taxes. It is important to be aware of these in case they ever apply to you, because you may need to plan differently so that you do not get stuck with a bunch of penalties and interest. As always, if you are unsure of your tax situation, consult with a tax professional.

Forgiven Debt

This is one that catches people by surprise every year. If a lender canceled debt due to a settlement, foreclosure, repossession, or loan modification, then you will likely be responsible for taxes on the canceled debt. In addition, if the loan was a secured loan and the collateral was sold to satisfy the debt, you may also have a taxable gain or loss to factor into your tax equation. There are exceptions for certain situations involving mortgages, student loans, bankruptcy, and other unique situations involving farms, real estate, and businesses.

If you are required to pay tax on forgiven debt, you will receive a form 1099 – C. This money will be included in your taxable income. Because the lender reports forgiven debt to the IRS, you do have to claim this money – otherwise you could find yourself facing audits and associated penalties and interest.

Forgiven debt is another area that gets terribly confusing for people, and another excellent time to reach out to a qualified tax consultant. The bottom line is that you do not want to get caught not paying taxes on forgiven debt!

Gambling Wins/Losses

Gambling winnings include income made from the lottery, raffles, horse races, casinos, and more. Both cash and prizes are considered gambling wins and losses. The IRS requires you to pay taxes on all of your winnings, just as they require you to pay taxes on all of your earned income. What is interesting is that winnings are only pinned to you when they are above a certain amount. These thresholds vary based on where, when, and how you won the money.

The bottom line is that if "The House" requires you to fill out a form that includes your Social Security number, you will receive a form W-2 and will have to report the income. If they do not take your Social Security number, you are technically required to track and report that income, though it is harder for the IRS to hold you accountable for those earnings. If you lose money gambling, you can claim those losses in your itemized deductions. However, the sum of your total losses cannot exceed the sum of your total wins.

Sean T. O'Hare, CPA

Alimony

Alimony is income of immense interest to the IRS. Alimony does not include child support, property settlements that produced no cash, or certain payments relating to property use or property maintenance.

For the person making alimony payments, there are some lovely tax benefits. Alimony payments are fully deductible. They are separate from itemized deductions, so they make a significant impact by reducing taxable income. There is an exception to the deductibility rule that involves child support payments. If you are responsible for unpaid or late child support, you may not be able to deduct alimony payments, as they will be considered child support payments. This is another one of those confusing situations where it is wise to consult with a tax professional!

The party that receives alimony payments is responsible for paying taxes on the income. Because the party making the payments reports the Social Security number of the receiving party, it is crucial to report alimony payments. If alimony payments are substantial, which they often are, the receiving party is also likely responsible for paying estimated taxes.

Child Support

Child support is neither deductible nor taxable. Typically, it is the man making child support payments to the woman – though times are changing and more women are finding themselves responsible for making child-support payments, so both genders need to pay attention to this! The party making child-support payments is not allowed to deduct the payments. The party receiving child support is not required to report it as income.

Child support is a big deal. It is highly regulated and if unpaid can turn into a ferocious legal matter. Failure to pay child support as agreed can result in aggressive collections by the state. Not only will your wages probably be garnished, but you may find yourself with property liens, bank account liens, and even the forfeiture of your tax refund. It may cause financial ruin and eliminate your ability to participate in the financial system on any other basis besides cash. Even though there is no tax benefit to making your payments, there are humongous consequences for avoiding them. If you are responsible for child support, please just pay it!

Court Awards/Settlements

Some court awards or settlements are taxable, some are not. Typically, it depends on why the litigation began in the first place. If it was related to wages, pension, or business, the cash is probably taxable. If it was a settlement due to physical injury or sickness, it is probably not taxable.

If the settlement is taxable, you will receive a form 1099 – MISC, or a modified W-2 if it was related to unpaid wages. Generally, when you are finalizing the settlement you can ask the court if the income is taxable or not and make plans accordingly. It is always better to be proactive and plan for taxes than it is to be surprised by a giant tax bill on April 15.

Tips

If part of your income is tips, you are required to report that income. Because tips are often paid in cash, it is difficult to track and difficult to enforce. Many people simply choose not to report cash tips, which has resulted in a variety of stiffly worded tax laws designed to capture people who take advantage of this loophole. The most targeted industry is the restaurant and hospitality industry. People who work as servers and bartenders are the most scrutinized because they are the ones that tend to make a good chunk of their income from tips.

The IRS considers both employers and employees responsible for reporting tips. Specifically, employees are required to report tips to their employers so that tax withholding can be calculated correctly. Not every employer complies with this requirement, which results in a huge problem for both the employee and the employer.

As the pressure increases to report tips, employers are cracking down and taking matters into their own hands. Gradually, employers are adopting the practice of either estimating tips based on sales, an average dollar amount per hour, or tracking tips made on credit card payments. For the most part, it is no longer possible for an employee to get away with not reporting their tips, though they may be able to get away with incomplete reporting.

Other Tax Traps

If you're self-employed, and your business is taxed as a proprietorship or partnership, you'll also owe self-employment tax on your business income. Self-employment tax replaces the Social Security and Medicare you and your employer would pay if you were a regular employee. (We'll talk more about these business entities in Chapter Three.)

Some types of income aren't taxed at the regular rate. For example, tax on "qualified corporate dividends" and most long-term capital gains is capped at 20%. Tax on "unrecaptured Section 1250 gain" (mainly from sales of real estate used in your business) is capped at 25%. And tax on "collectibles" (art, jewelry, etc.) is capped at 28%.

There's also a new 3.8% "unearned income Medicare contribution" on investment income for single taxpayers earning more than $200,000 and joint filers earning more than $250,000. (Doesn't "unearned income Medicare contribution" sound better than "tax"?) For purposes of this new rule, "investment income" includes interest, dividends, capital gains, rental income, royalties, and annuity distributions. You might be in the 35% bracket for regular income, but pay 23.8% on capital gains – even though there's no such thing as a "23.8% bracket" per se.

The bottom line is that "tax brackets" and "tax rates" aren't as simple as they might appear. Your actual tax rate on any particular dollar of income can be quite a bit higher or lower than your supposed "tax bracket."

Audit Paranoia

The second biggest mistake that people make in regards to their personal tax planning is nearly as important as the first, and that's fearing, rather than respecting, the IRS. Many Americans are simply afraid to take deductions they're entitled to, for fear of raising the proverbial "red flag."

But what does the kind of tax planning we're talking about really do to your odds of being audited? The truth is, most experts say it pays to be aggressive. That's because overall audit odds are so low, that most legitimate deductions simply aren't likely to wave "red flags."

Audit rates peaked in 1972 at one in every 44 returns. But lately they've dropped to historic lows. For 2012, the overall audit rate was just one in every 100 returns.

Roughly half of those centered on a single issue, the Earned Income Tax Credit for low-income working families. The rest focused mainly on small businesses, especially sole proprietorships – and industries like pizza parlors and coin-op laundromats, where there are significant opportunities to hide income and skim profits. In fact, the IRS publishes a whole series of audit guides you can download from their web site that tell you exactly what they're looking for when they audit you!

So, if you do get audited, what then? Well, if you've properly documented your legitimate deductions, there's little to fear. In fact, about 15% of audits actually result in refunds. (Another 20% result in no change either way.)

And if you lose? You'll get what the IRS calls a "deficiency notice,' which is simply a bill for more tax. If you still think you're right, you can appeal it to the IRS. If you don't like the result you get there, you can appeal to the U.S. Tax Court. There's even a "small claims" division for disputes under $50,000.

Just how aggressive can you get before risking actual penalties (as opposed to merely paying more tax)? You can avoid accuracy-related penalties if you have a "reasonable" basis for taking a position on your return. Generally, this means your position has more than one chance in three of being accepted by the IRS. You can file Form 8275 or 8275-R to disclose positions you believe to be contrary to law or regulations. But some advisors recommend not filing them. Why volunteer information that can attract unwanted attention? (Think of this as the tax equivalent of calling in an airstrike on your own position.)

Are you worried about getting in real trouble, as in criminal prosecution? Don't. Seriously. For fiscal year 2012, the Service initiated just 5,125 criminal investigations (up from 4,720 in 2011). That's an almost unimaginably tiny fraction of the 240 million returns they collect in a year. Out of those 5,125 investigations, they recommended 3,710 prosecutions (IRS investigators don't actually prosecute offenders themselves; they turn that job over to the Department of Justice.) There were 3,390 indictments and 2,634 convictions — the Feds don't take you to court if they're not already pretty sure they can win. In the end, just 2,466 lucky winners drew all-expense-paid trips to "Club Fed."

In the end, the average American really has nothing to fear from the IRS Criminal Investigations unit. As far as most of us are concerned, the IRS is just the federal government's collection agency, nothing scarier. You've got to do something really outrageous to draw one of those 5,000 investigations.

Sometimes, just changing how you report an item can dramatically change your odds of getting audited. For 2012, the IRS audited 3.6% of Schedule C businesses reporting gross income over $100,000. Yet for that same year, they audited just one half of one percent of partnerships and S corporations, regardless of how much they made. That suggests you can cut your odds of being audited by over 86% just by reorganizing your business.

Here's the bottom line. You should never be afraid to take a legitimate deduction. And if your tax professional does recommend you shy away from taking advantage of a strategy you think you deserve, ask them to explain exactly why they say so. And don't be satisfied with a vague reply that it will "raise a red flag." Remember, it's your money on the table, not theirs.

Personal Taxes Wrap-up

Naturally, it is not possible to cover everything related to personal taxes in one chapter. Because the U.S. tax code is so large and complex, it would take a very long book to cover everything – and there would still be confusion. Even though taxes are a pain in the neck, just keep in mind that paying them keeps the government in operation. Taxes contribute to things that you enjoy every day in your life, such as freedom, accessible public transportation, clean drinking water, roads to drive on, an abundance of foods to buy at the grocery store, and subsidized gasoline.

It is always good to visit with an accountant or tax consultant when your income situation changes. You need to be aware of the new forms to file and necessary changes to your tax strategy. For example, if you are switching from being employed to self-employed or retiring, a planning session with an accountant can make a huge difference in your strategy. It may help you learn how to reduce your liability and give you a bit of peace of mind. People who are going to experience a change in filing status may also want to get professional help the first time they file taxes in their new situation.

As a taxpayer, you have the right to either calculate and file your own taxes or take them to a certified preparer. Though it does cost money to have your taxes prepared, you can deduct those fees from the next year's taxes. Often, it is worth it to get professional help because the professional makes sure that you are getting the credits and deductions you deserve. Another option is to use a tax calculating program like TurboTax® or TaxAct®. While these programs are not as intuitive as a person, they too can help you capture all of your income, deductions, and credits.

Ultimately, you are responsible for correctly reporting your taxes, even if you have a certified preparer do them for you. The IRS and state tax agencies have the right to audit your return for any reason. It may be a random selection, or there may be something on there (like a math error) that raises red flags. Either way, if you are audited and found to owe, that is your responsibility. While you do have some recourse, it is limited.

The most important thing to remember with taxes is that you cannot avoid paying them, and you need to plan for them. Nobody wants to get stuck with a big, expensive surprise at tax time. If you are not able to pay your taxes, the problem will only get worse. Not only will that unpaid tax follow you for the rest of your life, but you will also get hit with penalties and interest. The results could be financial ruin or worse – jail. Unless you have lots of money to pay for high-profile attorneys, you should just plan on paying your taxes!

There are plenty of terrific resources out there to help you understand your taxes. In recent years, the IRS has gone to great lengths to make itself more approachable to the public. Their website is packed full of information, resources, forms, and calculators to help you determine what you are eligible for.

Investment Taxes

Remember earlier when we talked about the different ways that people earn money? In that chapter, the focus was primarily on income that was earned through work or business activity. This chapter focuses on a different type of income – the type of income made from investments. This type of income is considered passive, and the IRS handles it differently from active income. In fact, there are several forms and calculators that apply exclusively to investments!

If you've paid attention to the news during the last few years, chances are that you have heard a lot of debate about the tax called capital gains tax. The tax is not fundamentally controversial, yet it is a point of great friction between members of Congress. The right-leaning members of Congress usually argue to reduce or do away with capital gains tax. The left-leaning members of Congress view capital gains as a massive source of income for the wealthiest people and are concerned that it is not taxed enough.

The right argues that taxing capital gains is unfair and that it literally reduces the ability of "job makers" to create new jobs. Without going too deep into economic theory, understand that this concept is part of the trickle-down economy theory popularized by President Ronald Reagan. The idea is that the when the wealthy have more money, they invest it in businesses – which leads to more jobs, which then stimulate the economy. Low capital gains tax is an element of this theory.

The left argues that capital gains are a "rich man's game" and that capital gains must be taxed; otherwise the wealthiest people in the country would get away with paying virtually no taxes. While paying no capital gains tax would be a treat for people that make their money off investments, like Warren Buffett, it would have a number of negative impacts on the rest of the country. In the worst-case scenario, it could result in the collapse of the government due to lack of funding. In less-severe scenarios it would cause taxes for the working class to rise exponentially, effectively bankrupting the population.

Indeed, the argument for or against capital gains tax could literally go on for pages. In fact, college students write their entire dissertations on the subject. The objective of this chapter is not to argue for one point or another, but rather to educate you about the tax – how it works, who has to pay, and how it impacts you. Capital gains are, however, a fascinating economic subject – and one that causes mildly entertaining rhetoric, drama, and headlines to come out of Washington.

The fact is that capital gains tax plays a vital role in the American economy. It is a massive source of revenue for federal and state government alike. As with regular income tax, you need to have a basic understanding of capital gains tax – and be knowledgeable about what you need to do to prepare for it.

What Are Capital Gains?

Capital gains are money that you make as a result of an investment. An investment may be something like your home or personal items such as furniture or collectibles. More often it refers to investments such as stocks and bonds. Technically, everything you own is considered an asset and may produce capital gains. According to the IRS, if you sell something and profit from it, you have made capital gains and need to pay taxes.

For example, let us say you own a collection of somewhat ugly antique furniture. The furniture was given to you for free. One day, you get rambunctious and decide to restore and sell it. Little did you know that the items were part of a rare collection that is irresistible to collectors.

You invested in a couple cans of varnish ($30), a sanding block ($15), and some new hinges ($10) to make the furniture functional and beautiful. You sold the entire set for $2,000 to a neighbor. This means that you made $1,945 – not bad for a day's work! Though you sold the antiques for cash to a private party, the profit is technically taxable.

The above is an example of how capital gains may be made from possessions. Unless they are settling an estate or going through a divorce, few people go to the trouble to track and report capital gains of this nature. What is more common is for people to track and report capital gains made from investments and property. Though you are technically supposed to report all capital gains, the ones that the IRS really focuses on are those related to property investments. This is because they are documented and reported.

Dividends
Dividends are a little kickback offered by many stocks, as well as a financial benefit offered by many partnerships, estates and trusts, or by ownership in a corporation. Essentially, a dividend is a portion of the profits distributed (given) to an investor. The amount varies from investment to investment. The whole point of dividends is to add value by rewarding investors with regular payouts at regular intervals, typically quarterly – cash in the pocket is always nice. They may either be paid in cash or reinvested.

Reinvested dividends are often part of a DRIP (Dividend Reinvestment Program). Essentially, a DRIP increases the value of an investment exponentially because dividends are used to purchase more stock, rather than being paid in cash. This plan is not offered by every corporation, but many do choose to offer it to investors because it greatly enhances value.

When it comes to taxes, the dividends are considered a capital gain, and are therefore taxed – even when you never see the money.

DRIP investments can get quite complicated, and if not managed correctly can result in a lot of tax exposure. It is vital to understand how much you are making in DRIP dividends so that you can either pay estimated taxes or invoke some capital losses to reduce your potential tax liability. Do not hesitate to contact an accountant with expertise in investments to understand your tax liability.

Let's say that you bought 100 shares of Starbucks at $35 a share. You held the stocks for a year – a record-breaking year for the company. During that time there was a 3-for-1 split, so you now own 300 shares. The stock price is currently at $29 a share, and you decide to sell because it looks like the company is headed for rough times. You sell your stock and make $8,700. Your original investment was $3,500. Trading fees associated with the purchase and the sale were $15 each.

The original purchase is known as the "cost basis." There are actually several ways to calculate cost basis, which we will go into in a moment.

You realized (received or earned) a net gain of $5,170. Net gain = total sale price – cost basis – fees

You are now responsible to report and pay taxes on that the net gain of $5,170 to the IRS.

Capital Loss

When you sell a stock or an investment for less than you bought it for, you have a capital loss. It sounds like it is detrimental to lose money, but with investing there is a place and time for capital losses. Real estate and investments are eligible to claim capital loss. The amount is not calculated until the loss is realized (the sale is made).

An excellent example of capital loss is the housing market in between 2007 and 2010. Just about every home in the United States lost value, but people still had to buy and sell homes. If a seller sold a house for less than they owed on the mortgage, or less than they paid for it, a capital loss was realized.

The reason that capital losses are vital to investment strategy is a little tax deduction known as the Capital Loss Carryover. Capital losses may be deducted from capital gains, which reduces the amount of capital gains tax you will owe. Though limits change from time to time, you may typically claim $3,000 in losses in any given year. You can do this until you have exhausted the balance of the original loss. The carryover is limited to whatever the limit is for that tax year.

This means that if you realized capital gains of $3,000, and you had a carryover from the prior year equal to $3,000, your net capital gain will be zero dollars. If in the year 2013 you experienced capital loss of $20,000, you are likely going to be relieved of paying capital gains tax for several years into the future. Depending on your situation and the particular year's tax code, you may even be able to deduct capital losses from your regular income.

Successful investors know how to leverage the Capital Loss Carryover to minimize their exposure to capital gains tax. Though the carryover is limited, the fact that the balance can be carried forward forever makes it an irresistible tax strategy for investors.

Short-Term Gains vs. Long-Term Gains

Not all capital gains are alike. Specifically, there are short-term capital gains and long-term capital gains. The intent behind separating the two is to reward people who use a long-term investing strategy. Here is another area where the topic of capital gains gets a little dry and confusing.

Short-term Capital Gains: When an investment is held for less than a year, it is typically considered to be a short-term gain. Profits are typically taxed at your regular income rate, which is usually higher than the capital gains rate.

Long-term Capital Gains: If you hold an investment for more than a year, you are typically eligible to claim the lower capital gains tax rate on profits. For many taxpayers, capital gains tax is lower than income tax rates. The more money you make, the more relevant that is. However, the capital gains tax rate is subject to changes every year and varies based on the leadership and political climate.

As discussed in Chapter 6, investment accounts such as IRAs are subject to tax. These do not typically fall into short-term and long-term gains because when you start taking distributions, they are taxed as regular income. Essentially, you do not have to worry about calculating short-term versus long-term.

If you have a capital loss exceeding $3,000, you may carry the balance forward to the next tax year and capital gains taxes on qualified retirement accounts.

Important Things to Know about Capital Gains and Losses

Everything you own for personal use, pleasure, or investment is considered an asset, and subject to capital gains if you sell it and make a profit.

All earnings from capital gains must be reported on your tax return – technically even those made in cash and sold to private parties like your neighbor.

Capital losses may only be deducted on investments, not assets held for personal use. So the house and stock portfolio are eligible for capital loss, but the boat, timeshare, and RV are not. (Exception: Unless they are treated as investment property – but that's a whole different ball of wax because it is a business at that point.)

There are short-term and long-term capital gains. Short-term capital gains are taxed at the regular income level while long-term capital gains receive special treatment.

The Capital Loss Carryover may be used to reduce future taxes.

Capital gains and losses are reported on form 1040, schedule D.

Capital gains and losses can be quite confusing, especially if there are dividends, DRIPS, varying cost basis, and short-term and long-term gains to calculate. There is no shame in admitting confusion and seeking help from an account who has a thorough understanding of investment tax law.

Part V: Tax Debt

Sean T. O'Hare, CPA

Getting into Trouble with the IRS

"If you drive a car, I'll tax the street. If you try to sit, I'll tax your seat.
If you get too cold, I'll tax the heat. If you take a walk, I'll tax your feet."
-*Taxman*, The Beatles

The Beatles wrote from a satirical perspective in their song *Taxman*, but when you are filing your taxes, it can certainly feel like "they" are trying to tax your feet and your seat. However, it simply is not true. Taxation has come a long way from how it was handled in empires of the past.

Consider how the Romans collected their taxes.

In the mid- to late stages of the Empire, Rome would contract local citizens to collect taxes. These people were known as publicans. Their job was to collect taxes on behalf of the empire and send whatever was due back to Rome. The publican retained the balance of what he collected for his own personal gain. Could you imagine paying taxes to a third party that skims off the top?

The IRS, though an independent entity from the U.S. government, at least sends the money where it is supposed to go. Though there have been reports of private agencies such as major banks and hedge funds collecting taxes on property, the practice is pretty rare. When you make out a check to the U.S. Treasury, it is going to go to the Treasury.

Of course, that is of little comfort when sending a substantial chunk of your income away, but always remember that it does go to support some of the highest standards of living the world was ever known. There is little you can do about it. Taxes must be paid, or you pay the penalties. For most people, it is more desirable to pay them than to deal with penalties.

Mo' Money Mo' Problems

Notorious B.I.G. nailed it, didn't he? While the IRS sometimes appears to pick on small businesses and industries that deal in a lot of cash, the IRS really focuses on big income earners. Hollywood A-list celebrities and ultra-rich athletes are often selected for extra scrutiny. It makes sense, because these people are making millions and millions of dollars. When the IRS discovers an error on their tax return, it often results in millions of dollars for the Treasury. Here are some high profile cases of tax troubles:

Lindsey Vonn, the downhill skier who earned an Olympic Gold Medal, was found to owe over $1.7 million to the IRS in 2010. She took responsibility and worked to clear up the debts quickly. In interviews, she indicated that she felt it was her trust in her estranged husband that caused the troubles.

O.J. Simpson just cannot keep himself out of trouble. Between 2007 and 2011 he paid no taxes. It resulted in a tax bill of almost $180,000. Of course, when you are talking about a person of such notoriety, it is not a surprise that he also has tax troubles.

Lauryn Hill, a famous female rapper who rose to fame during the mid- to late 1990s, was found to have avoided income taxes for three years – even as she made $1-2 million. In May 2013, Lauryn Hill was sentenced to three months in prison for tax evasion. According to her, her decision was purposeful and intended to be a part of building an anti-military-industrial complex underground culture.

Martin Scorsese, acclaimed filmmaker, earned himself a $2.85 million tax lien in 2011. In true Hollywood style, he learned of his massive tax bill on Valentine's Day. Mr. Scorsese has been in tax trouble before, partially due to his relationship with the scandalous Ponzi-scheme running character, Kenneth Starr.

What Causes Tax Troubles

Tax troubles can begin as a small miscalculation that leads to underpaid taxes, or can be as big as purposefully avoiding paying taxes. There are many reasons that the IRS becomes alarmed and decides to look into tax returns, but the most common are pretty straightforward and easy to avoid.

Unfiled Returns

The IRS does not look kindly on people who do not file annual tax returns. Once you begin filing, it is rather difficult to explain why you stopped. This is especially true if you are making reportable income such as wages and salary or have received 1099s. If you are getting tax forms in the mail, so is the IRS.

If you do not file a tax return, the IRS will track you down. They will file the missing return and calculate taxes in the most advantageous way for them. The next time you go to file taxes, you will find there is a massive tax bill waiting for you.

Unpaid/Underpaid Taxes

If you do not pay taxes, but the IRS thinks you should have, they will find you. Not only will you be liable for the unpaid taxes, but you also be hit with penalties and interest that cause the balance to go up exponentially.

Underpaid taxes often result when the tax return is not calculated correctly, or certain information is purposely left out. This is where a lot of celebrities get caught up in tax troubles. Sometimes it is inadvertent – they simply forgot to report a portion of their income, or their accountant overlooked a detail. The same thing happens to working-class folks every year.

If you are in tax trouble with the IRS, the worst thing to do is nothing. The best thing to do is to respond promptly, professionally, and with the intent of settling the bill. To avoid making problems worse, keep complete records to prove every deduction and credit you claim, as well as records of your income.

Practicing due diligence when preparing returns is of crucial importance; it can prevent problems before they even start. Using tax calculation software or working with a tax professional is an excellent way to head off problems before they start. Being honest and reporting every penny you earn will also help you avoid problems.

Strategies for Avoiding Tax Troubles

Keep good records. Maintain paper or electronic records of every receipt, invoice, and payment made that is reflected on your tax return.

Quadruple check your math. Make sure your math is correct! Using a spreadsheet or tax calculating tools will help prevent human error.

Report all income. Pay especially close attention to W-2s and 1099s. These forms will come in the mail in January. Copies of these forms also go to the IRS, so reporting those numbers is crucial to staying out of trouble. If you work in a job where you make cash, such as a bartender, you need to report that income to avoid raising red flags.

File on time. Filing late is an easy way to raise eyebrows at the IRS.

Pay on time. If you owe taxes, be sure to send full payment with your return, or send what is feasible and apply for an installment plan.

Use the right forms. Be sure to read all of the literature associated with each form carefully to make sure it is the most appropriate form. If unsure, consult a tax professional or use a tax calculation program such as TurboTax® or H&R Block®.

Be consistent. If your income and reporting methods change vastly from year to year, you may bring unwanted attention to yourself. For most people, little changes from year to year are normal. Major changes without logical explanation increase the possibility of raising red flags.

Obtaining Tax Debt Relief

If you get notices from the IRS, get help from somebody who understands tax resolution. You might have all the loud ads on television making wild claims that they can settle IRS debts for "pennies on the dollar" and "get the IRS off your back." While they may be able to help, your best bet is to find a local Certified Tax Resolution Specialist (CTRS) to help you. The difference between the tough-talking television attorneys and a local CTRS is that your unique problems will get the attention deserved.

CTRS is a special certification awarded by the ASTPS (American Society of Tax Problem Solvers) to attorneys, CPAs, and other upstanding members of the financial community. It is a challenging certification to obtain and is the qualification to demand when hiring somebody to help you solve tax problems.

Major tax-preparation houses also offer audit services, but these are very different from services provided by a Certified Tax Resolution Specialist. Typically, their services stop at representing you and your records during an audit. A CTRS possesses the knowledge and experience needed to negotiate settlements successfully, release liens and levies, and handle problems that come up during audits.

Of course, you do not have to hire a professional to help you through your tax problems, but it can be incredibly time-consuming and stressful to "go it alone." When it comes to collecting tax debt, the IRS is essentially a big bully. They do not care why you did not pay your taxes, they do not care if it was an honest mistake, they do not care if it was your ex-spouse's fault. Worst of all, they do not have to follow normal rules; they collect with impunity, and the law is on their side. All they care is that you owe money. They will stop at practically nothing to get it from you.

For a review of your situation by a licensed CPA and a CTRS, give my office a call at **(207) 741-2400**.

Sean T. O'Hare, CPA

Liens, Levies and Wage Garnishments

Let's talk about all the horrible things that the IRS can do to you when you owe them money.

A Notice of Federal Tax Lien (NFTL) is an encumbrance that establishes a legal claim by the government. It does not result in the physical seizure of your property. A levy, on the other hand, allows the IRS to actually seize wages, cash, or property. Levies are normally divided into two categories. The first category includes tangible, real and personal property that you own. The second category includes third parties who hold property belonging to you such as bank deposits and wages.

The first category is often referred to as a "seizure", while the second category is usually referred to as a "levy" or "garnishment". The IRS must file a lien before they can issue a levy and must place a levy upon your property before they can seize your property. Levy action is the usually the most severe collections action the IRS takes against the majority of people that owe back taxes, and it is this type of action that an IRS employee is referring to when they talk about "enforced collection."

Federal Tax Liens

Once the IRS makes a valid assessment against you, the IRS is required to give notice and demand for payment within 60 days by law. If you don't pay the taxes owed, a Federal Tax Lien automatically arises and attaches to property and property rights either own directly by you or acquired after the date of the tax assessment. Both Federal law and state law are relevant in determining the effect of the Federal Tax Lien against you and your property. Federal laws determine whether the tax lien has validly attached and state law aids in determining to what property the lien attaches. Under your state laws certain property may be exempt from the lien.

In general, a tax lien gives the IRS a claim against everything you own, from your home and car all the way to the rusted bicycle in your backyard. The lien also technically attaches to your wages, money in your bank accounts, your retirement accounts, and even the cash in your wallet.

A Federal Tax Lien also impacts your credit score, since it shows up on your credit report. Therefore, the tax lien can impact your ability to obtain loans, rent an apartment, and can even impact your insurance rates and ability to obtain employment if you are a job seeker.

In most cases, a tax lien will jump ahead of many other liens against your property after a 180 day period, unless a particular piece of property is used as collateral for a loan. For example, a tax lien does not jump ahead in priority position over a car loan or a first, second, or third mortgage against your home. It will, however, usually jump ahead of, say, a mechanic's lien against your home.

You may have circumstances where having the lien released would be of benefit to helping you resolve the tax situation. There are three types of lien releases available to a taxpayer that may help you resolve tax liabilities with the IRS.

Certificate of Discharge

A Certificate of Discharge (COD) is the process of removing a single piece of property from being subject to the tax lien, usually so that the property can be legally transferred. For example, if you are trying to sell your house but the presence of the lien is preventing this from occurring, then you would need to obtain a Certificate of Discharge to release the tax lien against your house.

In the vast majority of cases, the IRS will not release a lien against a particular piece of property unless they are somehow going to benefit from it. They will generally approve a Certificate of Discharge if the lien discharge will facilitate the sale of the property in such a way that the IRS will get some money out of it. In other words, releasing the lien will facilitate collection of the tax.

If the government isn't going to see any money out of releasing a piece of property from the lien, it's possible to still obtain a Certificate of Discharge if there is a valid reason. In particular, if the IRS won't be receiving any money, but getting rid of the property will free up cash flow and put you in a better financial position in regards to your income and expenses so that later on down the road you can start paying on your taxes, then the IRS will likely approve a Certificate of Discharge.

If the property in question has no significant fair market value, the COD may also be granted, but this is much more of a hit-or-miss situation.

Lien Subordination

A lien subordination is the process of moving the tax lien down a notch in the prioritization of claims against a piece of property. For example, if you own a house free and clear, and the tax lien is in first position against the house, you can't obtain a mortgage against the house. No lender in their right mind is going to loan you money against that house unless their lien is going to take first position.

The answer to this problem is the lien subordination. The IRS will usually approve the subordination of their lien against a property if the lien that will be taking first position ahead of the tax lien will result in money going to your tax liability.

In the house example, obtaining a subordination of the tax lien in order to obtain a mortgage against the house will result in cash coming from that mortgage. At closing, that cash will go directly to the IRS, the mortgage will move into first position, and the tax lien gets re-recorded in second position.

Remember, paying interest on a loan is almost always going to be cheaper than paying penalties and interest to the IRS.

There are other conditions where a lien subordination will still be approved, even if the IRS isn't going to obtain direct proceeds from doing so. For example, many trucking companies will finance their accounts receivable through a process called factoring. In factoring, a lender pays the trucking company some percentage of their accounts receivable (usually 75% to 90%) up front, and then the lender takes the responsibility of collecting on that account receivable when it's due, usually 30 to 90 days down the road. This way, the trucking company gets money now so that they can buy fuel and make payroll.

When a tax lien is filed, most factoring lenders stop funding. In that case, the trucking company suddenly loses all it's cash flow. In order to enable the funding to continue, a lien subordination can be obtained that move the tax lien to a position below the factoring lender, thereby protecting the lender's claim on those accounts receivable.

Lien Withdrawal

There are rare occasions when obtaining an outright release of the entire Federal tax lien is actually the best way to progress towards a resolution of your tax liabilities. If a case can be made that the withdrawal of the lien will facilitate payment of the tax liability, or is otherwise in the best interest of both the taxpayer and the government, then the government may be open to this.

Another case where a lien withdrawal can be applied for is when you have entered into an Installment Agreement to pay the back taxes and the agreement did not mandate that a lien be filed, particularly a payment plan where the payments are directly withdrawn from your bank account. In these cases, you can often get the lien released as long as you are current with your payments and other tax obligations.

Certificate of Release of Paid or Unenforceable Lien

The IRS is required to issue a certificate of release of lien no later than 30 days after one of the following events occur:

1. The tax liability is paid in full.

2. The tax liability is no longer collectible. In other words, the 10-year statute of limitations on collections has expired.

3. The IRS accepts the bond of a surety company or payment of all taxes owed is to be made no later than six months before the expiration of the 10-year collection statute.

4. The taxpayer delivers a cashier's check to the IRS and receives a Certificate of Release of Tax Lien.

Bank Account Levies

An IRS levy is the actual action taken by the IRS to collect past due taxes. For example, the IRS can issue a bank levy to obtain your cash in savings and checking accounts or the IRS can levy your wages or accounts receivable, if you run a business.

The person, company or institution that is served the levy must comply or face their own IRS problems. For example, when the IRS issues a levy against your bank accounts, your bank must comply. The bank is required to take the funds out of your account to which the levy attaches on the day they process the levy. They must then hold those funds for 21 days and then after the 21 days, send those funds to the IRS. If they fail to do this, the IRS will come after your bank and penalize them. The additional paperwork that the bank or other company or institution is faced with to comply with the levy usually causes your relationship to suffer with the person or institution being levied.

When a financial institution receives a levy on your bank account, it cannot surrender the money until 21 calendar days after the levy has been served. This 21-day waiting period provides you the opportunity to notify the IRS and correct any errors regarding your accounts. An extension of this 21-day period may be granted by the Area Director of the IRS if there is a legitimate dispute regarding the amount of tax owed. Anytime during the 21-day waiting period the levy can be released. During these 21 days it is imperative that you exercise your appeals rights. In this case, you will want to file a CAP appeal. CAP stands for Collection Appeals Process. When you file a CAP appeal, the IRS must hear your case within five days. Please see the chapter on Appeals for more information about this process.

Levies should be avoided at all costs and are usually the result of poor communication with your Revenue Officer. When the IRS levies a bank account, the levy is only for the particular day the levy is received by the bank. As I mentioned, the bank is required to remove whatever amount of money is available in your account that day up to the maximum amount of the IRS levy and send it to the IRS after that 21 day hold period. This type of levy does not affect future deposits. So if your bank account gets levied today and all the money is taken out by the bank to be sent to the IRS 21 days later, you can make a deposit tomorrow that is not subject to that IRS levy.

An IRS wage levy is quite different. Wage levies are filed with your employer and remain in effect until the IRS notifies the employer that the wage levy has been released. Most wage levies take so much money from your paycheck that you don't have enough money to live on. In most circumstances, an IRS wage garnishment will take 70% to 80% of your entire paycheck. For most taxpayers, wage garnishments are the worst thing the IRS can do to them, and everything possible should be done to avoid this debilitating attack on your personal finances.

Personal Property Levies

The IRS's levy power is extremely broad and does not require that the IRS take you to court. The IRS can use its authority to gain possession of your property to pay any back taxes owed and all they have to do is file a notice in demand of payment, wait 10 days, then file a 30-day notice of intent to levy. After that 30 days, they can then levy. The effect of a levy is to compel you to turn property over to the IRS. Amounts that the IRS gains from a levy or garnishment are applied to your tax debt as follows:

The proceeds are applied to the expenses of the levy in sale.

Proceeds from the levy are then applied to the tax specifically relating to the levied property.

Proceeds are then applied to the delinquent tax liability that caused the whole situation in the first place.

Funds collected by a levy are considered to have been paid involuntarily. Therefore, you cannot specify to the IRS how you want those funds applied, which you are normally able to do if you make voluntary payments. This is yet another reason why levies are best avoided.

As we already mentioned, the IRS is required to notify you of its intent to levy you at least 30 days before the levy. This is done thru a notice called a Letter 1058 and states across the top of the notice, "Final Notice of Intent to Levy". When you are issued a Letter 1058 by the IRS, you have broad appeals right that allows you to appeal the proposed action. However, your appeal must be submitted within the 30 day window. If you've recently receive a final notice of intent to levy, please see the Chapter on Appeals to learn how to file a Collection Due Process appeal.

Seizures

The IRS must issue a notice of seizure to the owner of any real property (e.g. real estate) or the possessor of personal property as soon as practicable after the property is seized. This notice has the same effect as the Notice of Levy and can be delivered in person to the owner or possessor of the property or left at your home or normal place of business. Seizures must always be approved by upper IRS management. The supervisor must review your information, verify that the balance is due and affirm that a lien, levy or seizure is appropriate under the circumstances. Failure to give the proper notice will invalidate the seizure and afford you certain legal rights.

Seizures of your residence or business

The IRS is no longer really in the business of seizing homes and entire businesses. These sorts of seizures have become relatively infrequent, largely in due to the adverse publicity that the IRS has received from conducting these actions. The Taxpayer Bill of Rights prohibits the IRS from seizing real property that is used as a residence by the taxpayer for tax amounts of $5,000 or less, including penalties and interest. The Taxpayer Bill of Rights also only permits a levy or seizure on a principal residence if a judge approves of the seizure in writing. Following the 1998 Restructuring Amendments to the Internal Revenue Code, the process for seizing your home has become incredibly difficult for the IRS, which is a good thing for you.

Wage Garnishments

The IRS wage garnishment is a very powerful tool used to collect taxes owed by bringing your employer into the situation. A wage garnishment cannot only be an inconvenience and an embarrassment but it can also leave you with no money to pay your regular living expenses. Once a wage garnishment is filed with your employer, the employer is required to collect the vast majority of each of your paychecks and send that money to the IRS. As mentioned earlier, the wage garnishment will usually take 70% to 80% of your paycheck. In addition, if you receive Social Security, the IRS can take up to 15% of each and every one of your Social Security checks. The wage garnishment stays in effect until either the IRS is paid or the IRS agrees to release the garnishment.

A wage garnishment can be appealed through the Collection Appeals Program, just like a bank account levy. In addition, wage garnishments are a situation where seeking assistance from the Taxpayer Advocate can be extremely helpful.

Fair Debt Collection Practices Act

The IRS is subject to the conditions of the Fair Debt Collection Practices Act just like any other debt collector. This Act includes a number of rules controlling debt collection practices. Normally, these rules are to prevent excessive collections practices from being undertaken by collection agencies for things such as credit card debts and automobile payments. However, the Taxpayer Bill of Rights follows the Fair Debt Collection Practices Act guidelines and provides you certain rights.

For example, you cannot be contacted by a Collections Representative of the IRS outside of the hours of 8AM to 9PM, and it also prohibits harassing or abusive behavior from the IRS to you. The IRS may not communicate with you at an unusual time or place which is known or which should be known to be inconvenient to you. The IRS can also not communicate with you regarding your tax liability at your place of employment if the IRS knows or has reason to know that the your employer prohibits you from receiving such communication.

If the IRS knows that you are represented by someone who is authorized to practice before the IRS, then they can also not contact you. This provision does not apply if your power of attorney representative does not respond to the IRS within a reasonable period of time after being requested to do so. That is why it's important that if you hire professional tax resolution representation that you hire a reputable firm that's going to actually do what you pay them to do.

Tax Resolution Options

When you're trying to resolve tax matters with the IRS, you have a number of different options. Depending on your financial circumstances and the amount of your IRS back tax liability and other issues, you have several options available to you. In this chapter we will give you a brief overview of some of these options.

A Brief Word On Offers in Compromise

The Offer in Compromise is probably the most commonly known tax resolution strategy. This is what you hear about in TV commercials and radio ads, particularly when they talk about settling your tax debt for "pennies on the dollar" (a phrase which the IRS has technically banned advertisers from using). However, it is important to keep in mind that not everybody even qualifies for an Offer in Compromise, not to mention that this is only one of the many options that might be available to you. Each option must be explored in relation to the specific facts and circumstances surrounding your tax problem and then the best option can be selected and implemented. In some instances it may be necessary to employ two or more options to settle your tax obligations. Keep in mind that the ultimate goal is to solve your tax problem permanently and for the lowest amount allowed by law.

Big Option 1 – Full pay the tax owed

While seldom a popular option, sometimes you may have the ability to pay the tax outright or borrow against an existing asset, such as a cash out refinance of the equity in your home. Surprisingly, in this situation this option is usually the least costly of viable options available to you. The reason for this is simple. One, your equity and assets will usually disqualify you from benefiting from options which grant debt forgiveness. Second, until the tax debt is paid in its entirety it will continue to accrue penalties and interest. Generally, the combined penalty and interest rates that the IRS charges you are going to be significantly less than the interest rate you will pay from borrowing the money elsewhere.

Big Option 2 – Filing unfiled tax returns and replacing Substitute for Returns

When resolving a tax problem it is relatively common to have unfiled back tax returns. There are three reasons why it is necessary to file these returns and become current with your filing obligations.

Failure to file tax returns may be construed as a criminal act by the IRS and can be punishable by one year in jail for each year not filed. Filing unfiled tax returns brings you "current."

Filing unfiled returns to replace Substitute for Returns may lower your tax liability and the associated interest in penalties because the interest and penalties is calculated from the tax debt amount. A "Substitute for Return" (SFR) is when the IRS uses whatever information that they have available to them to prepare a tax return on your behalf. Now, most of the time this tax return that they prepare is not going to take into account your expenses, your credits, and any allowable deductions. In other words, an SFR prepared by the IRS based just on the copy of your W-2 that an employer filed with the IRS is not going to be in your favor.

A settlement cannot be negotiated with the IRS until you become completely current with all filing obligations.

Big Option 3 – Dispute the tax on technical grounds

If there is a technical basis to dispute the amount of tax owed, there are a number of paths to consider, such as filing an amended return if the statute of limitations to file has not expired or filing an Offer in Compromise under Doubt as to Liability criteria. If you are currently in an audit situation and the math on the audit is simply not right then you can contest the tax on these technical grounds by fighting for the correct calculations.

Big Option 4 – Currently Not Collectible Status

If you do not have positive cash flow above the level necessary to pay your minimum living expenses or you lack sufficient equity in assets to liquidate and pay the tax, you may qualify for Currently Not Collectible status (CNC). This is most commonly seen when you are either unemployed or underemployed. In this situation, the IRS places a temporary hold on the collection of the tax owed until your financial situation improves. If over a longer period of time your situation does not improve, you may eventually become a viable Offer in Compromise candidate.

Big Option 5 – Installment Agreements

In the vast majority of cases, the IRS will accept some type of payment arrangement for past due taxes. In order to qualify for a payment plan, you must meet set criteria, which includes the following, among other things:

You must file all past due returns.

You must disclose all assets that you own.

You must provide information regarding your monthly income and monthly expenses.

The difference between your monthly income and allowable expenses is the amount that the IRS will expect to receive from you under the payment plan.

Monthly payments can be expected to continue until the taxes owed are paid in full. However, it is possible to obtain a Partial Payment Installment Agreement (PPIA). A PPIA means that you'll have an Installment Agreement in place until the Statute of Limitations for collection of the tax expires. After the Statute of Limitations expires, the tax literally just goes away, along with all penalties and interest. The date on which the IRS can no longer attempt to collect the tax from you is called the Collection Statute Expiration Date (CSED).

Big Option 6 – The Offer in Compromise

The IRS Offer in Compromise program allows you to pay the IRS less than the full amount of your tax, penalties, and interest, and pay only a small amount as a full and final settlement. This program also has an option for Doubt as to Liability. In these cases you disagree with the amount of the tax assessment and this gives you a chance to file an Offer in Compromise and have your tax assessment itself reconsidered.

The Offer in Compromise program allows taxpayers to get a fresh start. In this process, all back tax liabilities are settled with the amount of the Offer in Compromise. Once the payment amount of the Offer in Compromise is fully paid off, all Federal tax liens are released. An Offer in Compromise filed based on your inability to pay the IRS looks at your current financial position, considers your ability to pay (income minus expenses), as well as your equity in assets. Based on these factors, an offer amount is determined. You can compromise all types of IRS taxes, penalties, and interest in one fell swoop. Even payroll taxes, which are often the most difficult to resolve, can be compromised. If you qualify for the Offer in Compromise program, you may be able to save thousands and thousands of dollars in tax, penalty, and interest.

Big Option 7 – Penalty Abatements

In most cases penalties can make up about 45% of your total tax obligation. A penalty abatement request can eliminate some or all of the penalties if you have reasonable cause for not paying the tax on time or paying the appropriate amount of tax. Reasonable cause includes the following: prolonged unemployment, business failure, major illness, incorrect accounting advice or bad advice from the IRS. To prevail in a penalty abatement request as in most tax matters, the burden rest with you to be able to adequately document the reasonable cause.

Big Option 8 – Discharging taxes in bankruptcy

Bankruptcy can discharge federal income tax if certain requirements are met. However, this depends upon both the type of bankruptcy and the type of tax owed. Chapter seven is the chapter of bankruptcy law that provides for the liquidation of non-exempt assets and the discharge of dischargeable debts. Chapters 11 and 13 provide for repayments of debt in whole or in part. To discharge taxes in bankruptcy, a number of criteria must be met:

Thirty-six months have lapsed from the tax return due date.

Twenty-four months have lapsed from the date the tax was assessed.

At least 240 days have passed since the tax was assessed and filing of bankruptcy.

All of your tax returns have to have been filed.

Big tax resolution option 9 – Innocent Spouse Relief

It is not uncommon to find yourself in trouble with the IRS because of your spouse or ex-spouses' actions. The IRS realizes that these situations do in fact occur. In order to help you with tax problems which are due to the actions of your spouse, the IRS has developed guidelines for you to qualify as an innocent spouse. If the taxpayer can prove that they meet these guidelines then the innocent taxpayer may not have to pay some or all the taxes caused by their spouse or ex-spouse.

Big tax resolution option 10 – Expiration of the Collection Statute

The IRS only has a limited time during which to collect back taxes from you. This time period starts on the date of the assessment of the tax and runs for 10 years. After the 10 years has lapsed, you no longer owe taxes, penalties or interest on that tax period. There are of course exceptions to this rule. You may agree in writing to allow the IRS more time to collect the tax. If you file an Offer in Compromise or if you file bankruptcy, these actions can both cause automatic extensions on the 10-year period. In these situations the amount of time for the IRS to collect the tax is extended usually by the amount of time that the action is in place.

So for example, if you file an Offer in Compromise and it takes six full months for the IRS to process your Offer in Compromise and give you a determination then the statute of limitations on collection is extended by another six months. If the IRS attempts to collect the tax obligation which is expired under the 10-year rule, the taxpayer must inform the IRS in writing that the statute of limitations has expired. Once this notification occurs the tax can be forgiven. So therefore, if you have tax liabilities that the IRS is trying to collect that are more than 10 years old, it is imperative that you calculate the exact Collection Statute Expiration Date, or CSED for short, and notify the IRS in writing that they are no longer allowed to collect on that tax if the date is passed the CSED.

The IRS Collection Information Statement

The Collection Information Statement is a financial instrument that the IRS uses to gather information to determine your ability to pay. This is a personal or business financial statement that gathers information regarding your assets, income, expenses and various other financial items.

Keep in mind that the IRS has established standards for allowable and necessary monthly living expenses. There are certain expenses that the IRS does not allow you to claim when preparing this statement and analyzing your financial condition. For example, the IRS disallows payments on unsecured debt such as credit cards. The IRS also does not give you credit for tuition, payments, 401K contributions or charitable donations. The national standards and local standards for necessary living expenses as set by the IRS consist of food, housekeeping supplies, apparel, and personal care products and services. It also includes housing, utilities, and transportation expenses which are adjusted based on regional differences.

Taxpayers are not required to provide documentation concerning the amount of expenses categorized as national standards for your corresponding income level. However, you are required to substantiate expenses categorized as local standards or other necessary expenses. Keep in mind that the IRS considers necessary expenses to only be those that provide for the health and welfare of you and your family or that relate to the production of income. These expenses must also be reasonable in amount. Some examples of other necessary expenses that the IRS may allow include child care, dependent care for the elderly and the disabled, other taxes, health care, court-ordered payments such as child support, secured debts such as you car payments, term life insurance, disability insurance, union dues, professional association dues, and accounting and legal fees for IRS representation.

The IRS Collection Information Statement is the primary form from which your eligibility for the various IRS resolution programs is determined. In particular, you will be required to provide this form to the IRS whenever you are applying for:

> Currently Not Collectible Status
> Offer in Compromise
> Installment Agreement

There are actually three different versions of the Collection Information Statement. In conversation, practitioners and the IRS refer to the form as just the "433", but the three versions do serve different purposes:

Form 433-F: The short version for individual taxpayers and married couples, used by the Automated Collection System (ACS) personnel that you talk to on the phone.

Form 433-A: The long version for individuals, married couples, and businesses that are sole proprietorships. The 433-A is used by field agents such as Revenue Officers, and also the version you should use when submitting an Offer in Compromise.

Form 433-B: The business version, used for all purposes when the taxpayer is a business other than a sole proprietorship.

The best way to look at the Form 433 is to think of it as a loan application. If you think of it in those terms, the form suddenly makes a lot more sense. In reality, it actually IS a loan application in many regards, especially if you are applying for an Installment Agreement to make monthly payments on your tax debt.

How To Fill Out Form 433

Each of the three different versions of the form have slightly different sections and questions. However, they are obviously more alike than different, even between the individual versus business versions.

The major difference between the Form 433-A and the Form 433-B is that the Form 433-A asks for information regarding your children and other dependents, and also about your employment information.

Warning! Providing the IRS with your current employment information gives them the information they need in order to issue wage garnishments!

The other big difference between the 433-A and B is that the income and expense portion of the Form 433-A for individuals includes a column for the Revenue Officer to fill in "Allowable Expenses". At the end of this chapter, we will go through an in depth explanation of allowable expenses, IRS National Standards, and disallowed expenses.

Note: If you run a business as a sole proprietorship or are self-employed, then you should fill out Form 433-A for your business. Pages 5 and 6 of the Form 433-A contain many of the same sections as the Form 433-B regarding the business operation.

Because of the similarities between the forms, and the fact that, as indicated above, the Form 433-A does actually contain business information sections for self-employed individuals, we're going to go through each section of the IRS Form 433-B, Collection Information Statement For Businesses, in order to give you detailed information regarding how to fill out each section.

Section 1 - Business Information: This section is pretty straight forward.

If you don't have information regarding the incorporation date, you can obtain that information from the Articles of Organization or Articles of Incorporation, available from the Secretary of State's office where the company was formed. This date should also be in the upper right corner of each year's business tax return.

For line 3c, frequency of tax deposits, this is specifically for businesses with employees. The vast majority of small businesses are required to deposit payroll taxes on a monthly basis, but some may have a large enough payroll to be required to make semi-weekly payments.

Lines 5 and 6 have to do with online payment processing and credit cards accepted by the business. If the company doesn't sell online, mark "no" for line 4, and leave line 5 blank. If the business accepts credit cards, fill in that information on line 6.

Section 2 – Business Personnel and Contacts: Please realize that whomever is listed as the "Person Responsible for Depositing the Payroll Taxes" may be investigated for the Trust Fund Recovery Penalty.

List the officers and owners of the business. Provide their Social Security numbers, home addresses, phone numbers, and what percentage of the business they own.

Section 3 – Other Financial Information:

This series of questions all require a yes/no answer. Check the appropriate box and provide the necessary explanation and other information for any "yes" answers.

For line 14, unless there is an actual event taking place, such as a major new client that will be paying the business a lot of money, mark this question as "no".

Section 4 – Business Assets & Liabilities:

My clients tend to overestimate the value of their assets. They often think in terms of what they paid for something and what it would cost to replace. However, for this section values indicated shouldn't even be Fair Market Value of the item, but actually should be the "liquidation value". Liquidation value is generally what something would sell for at auction.

The IRS wants assets information for a variety of reasons. For one, it is used in the calculation of an Offer in Compromise offer amount. Second, the IRS is looking for large value assets that you might be able to either sell or borrow money against in order to pay the IRS.

If you are still paying on any loans used to purchase the assets, be sure that information is included on the form.

Keep in mind that the Form 433-B is for a business – not yourself personally. Therefore, no personal assets should be listed on this form, only things actually owned by the business.

Specific line items:

#16 Bank Accounts - Indicate the name and address of the financial institution where you bank. Provide routing number (it will be nine digits), your account number and your current balance. Warning: Providing the IRS with your bank account information gives them the information they need in order to issues levies against your bank accounts!

#17, 18 Accounts Receivable - An Account Receivable is a customer that you did work for or provided products to, but they haven't paid you yet. Attaching a QuickBooks or similar printout is perfectly acceptable. If your business is a Federal government contractor, keep in mind that the Federal Levy Program will intercept any payments on your government contract and route that money to the IRS instead.

#19 Investments – Investments are things that could potentially be liquidated in order to pay the tax liability.

#20 Available Credit – List only lines of credit and credit cards that are in the name of the business, not in the name of an individual only. For credit cards, do not list trade or store cards, but only major credit cards such as Visa, Mastercard, and American Express.

#21 Real Estate: List any real estate owned by the business, how much it's worth, who the lender is, and how much is owed and the monthly payment. Also be sure to list property or commercial space that you rent, and include your lease information.

#22 Vehicles, Leased and Purchased: If it's got wheels and moves, list it here. That includes things like trailers, backhoes, airplanes, etc. For the value, I normally use Kelly Blue Book to find values of vehicles, and will look in trade publications, eBay, and Craigslist to get an idea of values for other types of equipment. If there is a loan or lease against the vehicle, include the lender, loan balance, and monthly payment.

#23 Business Equipment: These are large business assets that are bolted down. Again, be sure to provide loan information if any equipment is leased or financed.

#24 Business Liabilities: List here other loans not mentioned elsewhere on the 433-B. These will often be bank loans, Small Business Administration loans, notes, judgments, and other debts that aren't securing equipment or real estate.

Section 5 – Monthly Income and Expenses:

This section is also very important. The difference between the expenses and income is the monthly profit of the business. This amount is used in Offer in Compromise calculations, determines eligibility for Currently Not

Collectible status, and determines your monthly payment under an Installment Agreement.

In essence, this section is nothing but a shortened Profit and Loss statement. It is imperative that no expenses are omitted, so attach a Profit and Loss statement itself if necessary, or a listing of "Other" expenses for line #46.

Signature Block

Be sure to sign as a company officer by indicating your position within the company. Keep in mind also that you are signing this form under penalty of perjury.

Attachments Required

When representing a client, the single biggest impediment to obtaining a resolution of their tax liability with the IRS is obtaining all the supporting documentation that we need in order to properly work on their case. The vast majority of the time, I am inevitably submitted a Form 433-B for a client with large sections of the form blank and without significant supporting documentation.

The form itself, at the bottom, has a thorough list of what the IRS expects to see. Keep in mind that they expect copies of 3 months worth of any particular item, such as bills and statements.

Fortunately, the vast majority of the time a Revenue Officer doesn't complain about the lack of full supporting documentation. At an absolute minimum, just about every IRS Revenue Officer is going to absolutely insist upon receiving the following:

Copies of business bank statements for the last 3 months.

A Profit and Loss statement covering at least the last 3 months, but usually a Year To Date Profit and Loss.

At least one copy of a statement for each and every loan included on the 433-B.

In most cases, providing this minimum list of documentation will appease most Revenue Officers and Appeals Officers. If you are submitting the Form 433-B in support of an Offer in Compromise application and only submit this minimum list of supporting documentation, then you can expect a letter from the Offer in Compromise Process Examiner requesting all the information that you didn't include.

IRS National Standards and Allowable Expenses

As mentioned earlier, the income and expense section of the Collection Information Statement for individuals is quite a bit different than it is for businesses. Businesses are allowed to claim any reasonable business expense, and the Revenue Officer assigned to the case is allowed to (and often does) question any expenses that look fishy.

For individuals, though, the IRS sets very specific limits on what a household can claim as an expense, and also explicitly prohibits claiming certain expenses for collection purposes, including expenses that are deductible or create tax credits on a tax return. Many taxpayers are confused by this fact, and it is just one of the numerous inconsistencies across the tax code.

It should also be noted that the IRS National Standards are used by many other Federal agencies for various other purposes. The most common other purpose is that these expense guidelines are utilized by the bankruptcy courts for determining whether a bankruptcy filer ("petitioner") should be allowed to file for Chapter 7 bankruptcy or not (Chapter 7 is a liquidation of your assets and a "flushing" of your debts, whereas Chapter 13 is to set up a payment plan for several years to pay back your creditors).

Many people are shocked at how low some of the numbers are when they look at the National Standards. There are other people that are shocked, however, at how big some of the numbers are. Keep in mind that the IRS National Standards reflect the government's calculation regarding a precisely middle class existence.

For example, the allowable housing expense will vary geographically, because housing is cheaper in some parts of the United States, and much, much more expensive in other parts. However, the allowable expense for any area represents the median housing cost for that geographical area.

Summary

It is important to claim every allowable expense on your Form 433. Doing so will ultimately minimize the amount you end up paying the IRS on your back tax liabilities.

Confused?

We're here to help with your Form 433. We offer a special service to taxpayers in trouble whereby we will complete the Form 433 on your behalf and conduct a thorough analysis of your IRS records to help you determine your <u>exact</u> tax resolution options. To learn more about this service, please call my office at **(207) 741-2400**.

IRS Payment Plans

An Installment Agreement is a payment plan with the IRS to resolve back taxes. An Installment Agreement is by far the most common kind of IRS tax resolution obtained by taxpayers. In the vast majority of cases, the IRS will accept a payment arrangement for past due taxes. However, there are some qualifications that you have to meet first.

As we discussed in the last chapter, you have to have filed all your tax returns. It's okay if you owe money but you've got to file your tax returns. The IRS will require that you disclose all assets that you own, including all cash, bank accounts, and even retirement accounts. You must also demonstrate to the IRS that you do not have adequate cash available to pay the IRS. You must also not have the capacity to borrow the amount owed to the IRS from other sources such as a second mortgage on your home. You must also demonstrate that you don't have the money sitting in IRA's or 401K's. Keep in mind that the total dollar amount you owe usually dictates with whom you will be negotiating for an Installment Agreement.

If you owe the IRS less than $10,000 you can obtain what is called a Guaranteed Installment Agreement. A Guaranteed Installment Agreement can be obtained without ever talking to a human being. As a matter of fact, you can obtain a Guaranteed Installment Agreement right on the Internet. You must have all your tax returns filed, however and you must propose a payment amount of at least $25 per month. If you cannot make at least to $25 per month payment, the IRS cannot by law grant you a monthly payment plan. The Guaranteed Installment Agreement is a great way to go if your tax liability is under $10,000, particularly because this type of Installment Agreement does not require financial disclosure and you are not required to fill out any financial paperwork or provide bank statements or any other information.

Now, if your tax liability is more than $10,000 but less than $50,000, then you may be eligible for what is called a Streamlined Installment

Agreement. A Streamlined Installment Agreement also does not require financial disclosure via written forms and records. However, you will need to speak to an IRS Collections Representative that works in a call center called the Automated Collection System, or ACS for short. You can call ACS and obtain a Streamline Installment Agreement in most cases, within 30 or 45 minutes.

If you owe more than $50,000, chances are that you are dealing with an IRS Revenue Officer. A Revenue Officer is an IRS field collections agent. They will most likely ask you to complete a personal financial statement and if you have a business, you'll need to provide a business financial statement as well. The IRS determines allowable monthly expenses which will be matched against your actual monthly expenses. The difference between your monthly income and your allowable monthly expenses will be the amount that the IRS will require you to pay on a monthly basis.

Due to this financial review process, it often boils down to demonstrating the minimization of your income and the maximization of your allowable expenses.

When you're on an Installment Agreement, keep in mind that penalties and interest continue to accrue. This may cause you to be paying a large monthly payment to the IRS while your outstanding balance actually increases, since your payment may not even cover the monthly accrual of penalties and interest. Be careful because the IRS is most likely not going to explain this to you.

Installment Agreements are a widely used tool for tax collection. They're generally used when you're unable to pay the tax but you can pay enough each month to pay off the tax before the Collection Statute Expiration Date. If your Installment Agreement is one of the cases where the amount paid every month does not even cover the accruing interest and penalties, then you might want to consider an Offer in Compromise.

Obviously the IRS encourages you to pay what you owe as quickly as possible. If you are not able to resolve the tax debt immediately, an

Installment Agreement can be a reasonable payment option. Installment Agreements allow for the full payment of the tax debt in smaller, more manageable amounts. These amounts may be seasonally adjustable. For example, if you earn your entire living in a three-month period of the year based on the nature of your business, then the IRS may accept a Installment Agreement plan where you pay little or nothing during the other nine months of the year but make large payments during the three months of the year when you are earning income.

The amount of your monthly payment will be based on the amount owed and on your ability to pay that amount within the time legally available for the IRS to collect, which is that 10-year statute of limitations we've talked about in other prior chapters. If you enter into an Installment Agreement, the IRS may ask you to sign a waiver which extends the legal maximum time for the IRS to collect. If you have an Installment Agreement already in place for a previous tax liability, you still may be able to get help. All of the amounts owed could be included in one Installment Agreement. A collection information financial statement is most likely going to have to be provided to further illustrate your financial situation.

Now, here's a kicker about Installment Agreements. In future years, if you're on an Installment Agreement and file a tax return that ends up in a refund, the refund is going to be taken by the government. You're never going to see that money. So you're not going to get all of your refund if you owe past due amounts. This can even apply to state taxes, student loans, or child support. It is not uncommon for taxpayers that are behind on child support to have the IRS seize their refund. The IRS will automatically apply refunds to whatever taxes or other items are owed. If the refund does not take care of the tax debt then your Installment Agreement will continue on until all of the terms are met.

As mentioned before, if you owe less than $50,000 to the IRS, you may be eligible for a Streamline Installment Agreement. A Streamline Installment Agreement requires that the entire amount of the tax penalties and interest to be paid in less than five years and you are generally going to be required to make even monthly payments even if you have sufficient assets to pay the tax in full. Streamline Installment Agreements are usually negotiated without the need for full financial disclosure. These installment agreements are limited to taxes on income.

Once the Installment Agreement is in place, you must file all tax returns in the future on time. If you are unable to make an Installment Agreement payment as agreed, you should immediately notify the IRS to avoid levies or wage garnishments. If you default your Installment Agreement, the IRS will generally issue a final notice of intent to levy within 30 days. Once you default on a payment plan, it is very difficult to obtain another one, although it is possible.

When you enter an Installment Agreement, the IRS is going to collect a user fee. This fee is taken out of your first payment. If you signed up to have a direct debit taken out of your bank account, they'll charge you a $52 fee instead. The user fee drops to $43 if your income is below certain U.S. Department of Health and Human Services poverty guidelines. If you qualify for the reduced user fee of $43, the IRS will automatically adjust this for you.

Keep in mind that with an Installment Agreement, interest and penalty accrual does not stop. The interest rate on a loan or a credit card is generally lower than the combination of penalties and interests imposed by the Internal Revenue Code. Therefore, if you have the ability to borrow against a credit card or a loan in order to pay off your tax liability, it may be better and cheaper for you to do that in the long run.

In order to stay current with your Installment Agreement payments, the IRS suggests doing either a payroll deduction or direct debit out of your checking account. These forms of payment help to reduce the burden of mailing payments, saves postage, helps ensure timely payments and decreases the likelihood that the agreement will default. It is not uncommon for the IRS to lose payments that you mail in. Installment Agreement payments can be made by electronic funds transfer, credit card via officialpayments.com, personal or business check, money orders and cashier's checks.

However, never send cash through the mail.

The IRS generally will still file a Notice of Federal Tax Lien to secure the government's interest in your personal property until the final payment of your Installment Agreement is made. If you enter into an Installment Agreement, the tax lien is not released until the tax liability is paid in full or the collection statute runs. Keep in mind that the Notice of Federal Tax Lien can have a negative impact on your credit rating.

Generally, IRS enforced collection actions such as levies and wage garnishments are not made while an Installment Agreement request is being considered or while it is in effect. Collection action is also not generally taken for 30 days after a request has been rejected or an Installment Agreement is terminated. Once you have an Installment Agreement in place, it is really important that you make all your payments on time. If you can't make your payments on time due to some change in your financial status, you should contact the IRS immediately. The failure to make timely payments could default the entire Installment Agreement. A defaulted Installment Agreement could subject you to enforced collection action.

By law, the IRS is required to send you an annual statement of your Installment Agreement activity. This statement must provide the amount owed at the beginning of the period, the payments posted to the account, any fees or assessments added and then the annual balance. Typically, the IRS will send this annual statement to you every July.

Besides making installment payments on time, the terms of an Installment Agreement will always dictate that you file all tax returns on time and that you make any other required tax payments due during the life of the agreement on time as well. These payments would include estimated tax payments or Federal tax deposits for payroll taxes.

Guaranteed Installment Agreements

Whenever you see tax resolution firms advertise, you'll usually see a qualifier in their ad that says something to the effect of, "If you owe the IRS at least $10,000, then give us a call." The reason for this is that if you owe the IRS less than $10,000, there is a provision in the tax code that REQUIRES them to accept your proposal to pay them in monthly installments if you meet certain requirements. In fact, you don't even need to provide them with financial statements to qualify.

To qualify for a guaranteed installment agreement, you must:

Owe only income tax, not any other types of tax.

Have properly filed and paid all tax returns during the 5 years prior to accumulating the tax debt.

Not be able to pay the tax immediately out of savings or other means.

Pay the tax fully within 3 years (e.g., the payment plan cannot exceed 36 months).

File and pay all tax returns on time during the period of the installment agreement.

Not have had an active installment agreement during the past five years.

Owe less than $10,000 in TAX, not including penalties and interest.

Another beautiful thing about guaranteed installment agreements is that the normal legal minimum monthly payment of $25 per month does not apply. Yes, you can actually offer payments of $10 per month, and as long as that will fully pay the debt within 36 months, they have to grant you the request!

Lastly, guaranteed installment agreements can be granted by the lowest level collections employees of the IRS without managerial approval. All you have to do is make one phone call to the Automated Collection System (ACS), wait on hold for an hour, talk to a human for 10 minutes, and you're DONE.

Do keep in mind, however, that penalties and interest continue to accrue during these - and all other - Installment Agreements, although they are guaranteed by law. Because of this, you may decide it is in your best interest to fully pay any balances due as soon as you possibly can.

To set up your guaranteed installment agreement, contact ACS at one of these numbers:

Businesses: 1-800-829-3903

Individuals: 1-800-429-7650

Streamlined Installment Agreements

While not as "easy" as a Guranteed Installment Agreement, there is another provision in the tax code for taxpayers that owe less than $50,000. A Streamlined Installment Agreement is so called because there is a very, very streamlined process for obtaining one.

These agreements also do not require managerial approval by the IRS. If you owe slightly more than $50,000, it can often be advisable to do whatever you can in order to pay the balance down to less than $50,000 so that you can qualify for the Streamlined program.

The Streamlined Installment Agreement has two very beneficial components to it. First, you are not required to file a Form 433-A or B, or provide any other financial information. Second, you can obtain this payment plan even if you otherwise have the financial means to full pay your tax liability, but simply don't want to spend the cash all at once or liquidate assets or borrow against them in order to afford the full payoff.

To qualify for a Streamlined Installement Agreement, you must:

> Owe less than $25,000 in total TAX, not including penalties and interest.

> Owe only income taxes if you are an individual or a business that is still operating (if your business is closed, ALL tax types are eligible, including payroll taxes).

> Can pay off the full tax liability within 60 months or before the CSED.

As with all Installment Agreements, you must make all your payments on time and file all tax returns on time, paid in full, during the course of the payment plan.

If you enter into a Streamline Installment Agreement before a tax lien is filed, you can often avoid the filing of the Notice of Federal Tax Lien.

As always, penalties and interest still build up during the course of making payments on this payment plan.

Partial Payment Installment Agreements

A Partial Payment Installment Agreement (PPIA) is a payment plan where you will be making payments until the Collection Statute Expiration Date, but the entire tax liability won't be paid off. In many ways, this is similar to one of the payment options for the Offer in Compromise program. This option did not used to exist for taxpayers, but was created as an option under the American Jobs Creation Act of 2004.

Under IRS regulation, the agency will not normally ask a taxpayer to sign a document authorizing the extension of the CSED when an Installment Agreement is granted. The lone exception to this regulation is a PPIA, but even this is only in certain situations.

When requesting this type of payment plan, the IRS will closely scrutinize your assets. If you own anything that you can borrow against or sell and put that money towards the tax liability, the IRS is going to require that you at least attempt to sell or borrow against those assets.

PPIA's will require extensive financial documentation, including a full Form 433 and complete supporting documentation. Also, a Notice of Federal Tax Lien will definitely be filed against you if it hasn't been already.

If you are a candidate for a PPIA, and lack significant equity in your assets, then you may also want to consider applying for an Offer in Compromise. You may end up paying less under one program or the other, so they are both worth considering under these circumstances.

Delayed Collection... Perhaps Indefinitely

IRS policy states that whenever a taxpayer raises a question or presents information creating reasonable doubt as to the validity of a tax liability, reasonable forbearance will be exercised with respect to collection efforts as long as the interests of the government are not jeopardized. Now, this doesn't mean that your tax debt is going to be forgiven, or that the tax lien is going to be released, or that interest and late payment penalties don't continue to accrue. What it does is that it suspends collection action until you have the ability to actually pay the tax.

A very powerful tool for getting the IRS off your back is Currently Not Collectible (CNC) status. The IRS recognizes that you maybe in a financial condition that renders you unable to pay anything on your taxes. When I represent taxpayers that are either insolvent or are having major cash flow issues, the Currently Not Collectible Status is the option that we attempt to obtain most often.

If you have negligible assets subject to levy enforcement by the IRS and you have no income beyond what is absolutely necessary for you to live, the IRS may determine that your liability is currently uncollectible. Currently Not Collectible status defers collection action under the undue hardship rule. If you are one of these uncollectible cases, the Revenue Officer assigned to your case will remove your case from active inventory until your financial condition improves. Currently Not Collectible Status is generally maintained for about one year. There are many reasons the IRS may close your case as uncollectible. These include:

The creation of undo hardship for you, leaving you unable to meet necessary living expenses.

The inability to locate any of your assets.

The inability to contact you.

You die with no significant estate left behind.

Bankruptcy or suspension of business activities with no remaining assets.

Special circumstances such as tax accounts of military personnel serving in a combat zone.

Do keep in mind that if you are in Currently Not Collectible Status, penalties and interest will continue to accrue on your tax liabilities.

Before closing your case for the reason of undue hardship, I guarantee that the IRS will request a financial statement from you so that they can review your finances. The review is similar to the review for an Installment Agreement request and both of these items are similar to a mortgage application. You will be required to provide similar financial documentation such as bank statements, copies of mortgage statements and car payments, pay stubs, etc. If your assets are negligible and your net disposable income is negligible, you'll most likely to be able to obtain a CNC status.

The IRS will periodically re-examine your finances to see if your financial condition has improved to the point that some payment can be demanded. This financial review will occur about once a year and you must then complete a new financial statement. The IRS may question you by phone or in person about your updated financial information or they may simply send you the form and request that you return it by mail.

As with all information you give the IRS, make sure that what you say is absolutely truthful. The IRS may also monitor your financial condition by computerized review of your tax returns. For example, the IRS computers may flag your return if your reported gross income exceeds some pre-established amount. Remember, the IRS only has 10 years from the date of assessment to collect delinquent taxes; once the statute expires, so does your liability.

Millions of Americans have remained in CNC for years and completely avoided having to pay their back taxes. Obviously, these folks could not title assets in their own name or have significant income available for IRS levy. Still, many of these uncollectible cases enjoyed relatively comfortable lifestyles. If you maintain no assets in your own name, you have a small income, and expect your financial situation to continue, then remaining in CNC status may be your most practical remedy. However, if you do not intend on remaining uncollectible until the statute of limitations expires or you don't want the tax liability hanging over your head, then you may want to consider an Offer in Compromise while your financial situation isn't so great.

Taxpayers have been able to get Offers in Compromise accepted while being in CNC for literally just a few hundred dollars when they've been able to borrow the money from friends or family members strictly for purposes of settling the tax debt under the Offer in Compromise program.

Your Revenue Officer has the authority to place you into CNC. While declaring your accounts non-collectible does not eliminate the assessment, it does stop current efforts to collect the tax, and stopping enforced collection action is typically your overall objective. Collection can resume anytime before the end of the 10 year statute of limitations expires.

The decision by the IRS to place an account in Non-Collectible Status is generally based upon the information on your financial statement and this information must be no more than 12 months old. The IRS can place you in Non-Collectible Status even when you're financial statement reflects assets or income which can be levied as long as the collection of the delinquent taxes would prevent you from affording necessary living expenses.

Remember, your situation is unique. Factors such as health and age are considerable by the IRS. If you can make monthly payments of at least $25 per month, the IRS will most likely require to you enter an Installment Agreement.

Sean T. O'Hare, CPA

Settling For Less Than You Owe

Whenever you hear the phrase "pennies on the dollar" in relation to tax resolution, you are hearing a reference to the Offer in Compromise (OIC) program.

The OIC program is intended to give taxpayer's without the financial means to pay their tax debt to pay whatever they have, and then start over. In many ways, an OIC is akin to a bankruptcy filing on taxes only. The major difference, however, is that an OIC is an administrative proceeding, rather than a court proceeding.

An Offer in Compromise application will require complete financial disclosure. In other words, a full and accurate Form 433-A or Form 433-B will be required, along with complete supporting documentation. Because the government is going to accept less money for the tax debt than what you owe, they are going to go to great lengths to make sure that you actually qualify.

You should note that almost 80% of all Offers in Compromise are ultimately rejected by the IRS, either via the Offer process itself, or in Appeals. The biggest reason that Offers are rejected is because the applicant simply wasn't eligible for the program.

Some taxpayers file an OIC simply to "buy time" to figure something else out, since the process normally takes 6 to 9 months for an Offer application to be processed and denied, including Appeals. While this may be a worthwhile strategy for you, you should note the CSED is extended day-for-day while your Offer is in process, and for 30 days after it is ultimately denied.

Sean T. O'Hare, CPA

Eligibility

Your eligibility to settle for less than what you owe is directly related to your offer amount (see "Offer Calculation"). If your offer amount is equal to or greater than the minimum amount calculated using the IRS formula, then you may be eligible to file an Offer in Compromise.

Like other resolution options, the IRS also requires that you:

Have filed all past due tax returns

Are not currently generating new tax liabilities

Agree to properly file and pay on all tax returns, on time, for the next 5 years

Agree to let the IRS keep any tax refunds you would otherwise be due during the time you are paying on the OIC

Failure to abide by these rules will either result in rejection of your offer, or default of your offer agreement and reinstatement of any tax liabilities that were eliminated.

Payment Options

In addition to an application fee, you are required to make payments on the Offer in Compromise unless you meet low income qualification guidelines for an exception to this rule.

The first payment option is used when you will pay the entire amount of your settlement offer in 5 monthly payments or less. If you use this option, you may pay the entire offer amount when submitting your application, or include a minimum 20% deposit (non-refundable!) and take up to a maximum of 5 more monthly payments to pay off your Offer

– *after* it has been accepted. Using this payment option provides the benefit of not being required to make regular payments on your Offer while it is being processed. Using this option also generally results in paying the smallest possible Offer amount.

The second payment option requires you to make regular payments on your Offer in Compromise while the IRS is considering it. These payments are non-refundable, and the first payment needs to be included with your offer application. The second payment option requires that you pay off your entire Offer amount within 24 months.

Regardless of the payment option you use, your payments must add up to the total offer amount, and your offer amount must be at least your Reasonable Collection Potential (RCP), discussed next.

Keep in mind that penalties and interest continue to build on your tax liability while you make Offer payments, even though ultimately those penalties and interest go away when the Offer is paid off and settled. If you default on your OIC, however, those built up penalties and interest are added back on to your balance and you will be liable for it.

Offer Calculation

Many unlicensed tax resolution salespeople, either through ignorance or simply gross incompetence, will tell everybody that they talk to that they qualify for an OIC, and that the Offer amount is some percentage of what they owe.

In addition to this horrifically unethical practice, many tax resolution firms will also only tout their most successful OIC applications, showing you that they did indeed get 1.2 cents on the dollar for one client, and 4 cents on the dollar for another client, all while failing to inform you that:

a. Most of their OIC applications for clients were outright rejected, and

b. of those that were accepted, it was usually only for 50 or 75 cents on the dollar.

The Offer amount is the single most important part of a successful OIC application. Calculating the OIC offer amount is extremely formulaic, and requires a complete and accurate Form 433 to be filled out.

In fact, here's the single biggest secret to all but guaranteeing that your Offer in Compromise will be accepted:

Use the IRS formula, like you're supposed to anyway, to calculate your Offer amount.

The IRS goes through an extensive investigation phase to verify information on your Form 433, looking for other assets you own and income you failed to disclose. The IRS looks at various public records sources, and may even pull a credit report to verify what you've told them (this action doesn't require your direct authorization to the IRS under Federal law).

Within the IRS booklet containing the OIC application, there are versions of the Form 433-A and Form 433-B that are modified slightly for OIC purposes. If you use the PDF version of the booklet (search for "IRS Form 656B"), the calculations are actually carried forward for you to the lines that determine your Offer amount.

The entire purpose of these calculations is to arrive at what the IRS calls your "Reasonable Collection Potential", or RCP. The RCP is the sum of the net worth of your assets plus all of your disposable income for the next 1 or 2 years. In other words:

Settlement Amount = (monthly disposable income x a number of months) + the net realizable equity in the taxpayer's assets)

Disposable income is monthly income minus allowable monthly expenses. It is important to recognize that the IRS will not allow all expenses that you may actually have. Common disallowed expenses are college tuition payments for a dependent and church tithing. For more information on this topic, refer to the chapter on IRS Collection Information Statements.

The number of months over which disposable income must be calculated into the offer amount is based on the smaller of the number of months remaining until the Collection Statute Expiration Date (CSED) for the tax debt OR either 12 or 24 months, depending on the payment option for the OIC which the applicant is selecting.

"Net realizable equity in assets" is the quick sale value of the asset (often 80% of Fair Market Value (FMV)) minus any liabilities which are secured by the asset (e.g., a loan). As an example, if a taxpayer has a home worth $100,000 and owes $50,000 on the home, the IRS will calculate the net realizable equity in the asset as follows: ($100,000 x .80) - $50,000 = $30,000. The IRS expects, in this example, that the $30,000 will be included in the Offer amount.

Based on this explanation of how RCP is determined, and understanding that RCP is your minimum offer amount, I hope it is apparent as to why the IRS rejects so many OIC applications. In reality, the best OIC candidates are folks that have very little in the way of assets, and no disposable income. The best OIC candidates often tend to be unemployed and broke.

Application Process – What To Expect

When you file an OIC, a Process Examiner will look over your paperwork to make sure that the offer is "processable", meaning that you met all the administrative requirements to be eligible, properly filled out the forms, crossed your t's and dotted your i's, filled out a complete Form 433, and have filed all your tax returns.

If your Offer is deemed to be not processable, it will be returned to you with a letter from the Process Examiner explaining what you need to correct, and to resubmit your offer with those corrections.

If considered processable, an Offer Examiner will then be assigned to actually review the merits and financial aspects of your application. This is the person that verifies assets, orders credit reports, and basically gets very up close and personal regarding every aspect of your financial situation or the financial health of your business.

The Offer Examiner will usually provide you the opportunity to address any inconsistencies they discover in their findings, and to argue on your own behalf for the inclusion or exclusion of certain assets or expenses. More often than not, this is the phase where having a professional representative comes in handy the most, to handle these negotiations for you.

Once the Offer Examiner has all the information they need to either accept or reject your Offer, they will do so, and send you a letter explaining why.

Keep in mind that for Payment Option 2, you must continue to make monthly payments on your OIC while this review process is going on. If you fail to do so, your offer will automatically be rejected, and the IRS will keep the money you did pay and apply it to your tax liability as they see fit.

Appeals

If your OIC is rejected, you have the right to know why, and also the right to Appeal this decision. More often than not, a dispute over including an asset or expense item will be the argument you take to Appeals. Appeals Officers have the authority to accept or reject an OIC based on their own findings, rather than the findings of the Offer Examiner.

Reducing and Eliminating IRS Penalties

There are a lot of common misconceptions surrounding the abatement (removal) of IRS penalties and interest.

First of all, it is important for anybody that owes the IRS money to understand that you will not have interest charges removed. If somebody is trying to sell you on their tax relief services and they tell you that they can have the amount of interest on your tax account reduced or eliminated, they're lying. The provisions within the U.S. tax code for eliminating interest charges on back taxes are extremely limited and extremely specific, and if you owe the money but just simply couldn't or didn't pay it, you DO NOT qualify.

The second thing to understand is that the removal of any penalties is extremely formulaic. You must meet one of the reasonable cause criteria outlined by the Internal Revenue Code. Fortunately, these reasonable cause criteria are much broader and more applicable to more people and businesses than are the criteria for interest abatement. Some of the possible reasonable cause criteria include death or illness in the family, loss of records, and receiving bad advice from a CPA.

It is important to note that the two most common causes for accrual of a tax liability are not considered reasonable cause by the IRS, and most often you will not be able to have penalties reduced for these two reasons. These reasons are:

1. Ignorance of filing or deposit requirements
2. Cash flow problems that leave you without enough money to pay the tax when due

Under special circumstances, the IRS will grant penalty relief due to economic hardship, but it is a hard case to prove and tends to be a longer, more drawn out process through the Appeals division. The granting of this sort of penalty relief can also depend upon which Circuit Court of Appeals district you live in, since different case law has been interpreted in a different court jurisdictions.

Above all, just remember that you can get penalties abated, if you have a good reason that was beyond your control and that can be backed up with proper documentation. And as far as interest charges go – forget about it, the IRS is not going to let you off the hook for those if you actually do owe the tax.

One of the biggest things I am adamant about is correcting the myths, lies, and half-truths perpetuated by unlicensed tax resolution salespeople, and the IRS penalty abatement is one of the things least understood and grossly over-hyped by salespeople in our industry.

The "we can remove interest charges" lie, as mentioned at the start of this chapter, is one of the biggest lies that tax resolution sales people tell their propsects.

There are two, and precisely two, instances in which interest is reduced:

1. An IRS employee gives you false information, which you acted on and resulted in the interest. This is one reason why all IRS correspondence should be conducted and followed up in writing.

2. Since interest is calculated based on the tax liability, if an amended return is filed and the tax itself is lowered, then the interest is also reduced.

Reasonable Cause Criteria

Now, on to penalties. The IRS charges dozens of different types of penalties, but the three that we most commonly talk about are the late filing penalty, the late payment penalty, and the penalty for not making Federal Tax Deposits. These three penalties combined can add a whopping 65% to your total IRS bill. If your tax debt is more than two years old, you've maxed out all these penalties, and therefore over half your total debt is penalties.

The IRS does actually have a compassionate side, and it's generally found in the penalty abatement process. Penalty abatement applications can also be appealed if initially denied, so you can always get a second set of eyeballs on the issue. The thing to keep in mind is that the IRS has very strict guidelines for granting penalty abatements, and these guidelines are referred to as "reasonable cause criteria".

As mentioned earlier, "we didn't have the money" is NOT a reasonable cause criteria. A drop in revenue, by itself, is insufficient argument for obtaining penalty relief. Any request for penalty abatement simply citing the economic recession will be immediately denied.

Why is this? Here is the IRS' logic: You made the money, and should have paid the taxes at the time on that money. If you are self-employed and receive a check, then you HAD the money, you simply didn't give the IRS their chunk of it.

Same goes with payroll taxes for businesses, particularly the trust fund taxes (money you withhold from employee paychecks for income tax and Medicare/Social Security): If you had the expectation to pay some amount of wage, then you theoretically HAD the money sitting somewhere to pay that person, and should have withheld it and turned it over to the IRS. If you couldn't cover the taxes, you shouldn't have had the employee and should have laid people off or cut back their hours.

There are ways to argue around this, and we have done so very successfully, but there has to be some other circumstance. For example, you had the money to pay the tax, but paying the tax instead of something else would have created an "undue hardship".

Examples of "undue hardship" could include a large medical expense that unpaid would have left a condition untreated, or a court ordered payment that, if missed, would have resulted in other legal consequences, or a bill such as a large automobile repair which would have left you unable to get to work and resulted in job loss.

These arguments are difficult to make and require significantly more work than standard reasonable cause criteria applications, but they CAN be won, especially in the Appeals process.

The primary IRS penalty abatement reasonable cause criteria center around natural disasters, loss or destruction of vital business records, bad advice from the IRS or an accounting professional, criminal activity, medical issues, substance abuse problems, and other serious circumstances.

A couple years ago I developed a standard list of questions to ask clients to assist me in preparing their penalty abatement. This list of questions should be given some serious thought before requesting penalty abatement, as you are more likely to get what you want if your request covers one of these areas:

Were any financial records lost or destroyed?

Was there any transition in your business that lead to the failure to pay taxes, such as a change of ownership?

Was there a death or serious illness that directly affected your ability to work or impacted the operation of your business?

Were you the victim of any embezzlement of funds, theft of valuable property, or identity theft?

Were there any alcohol or drug abuse issues that affected your business or your personal wage earning capability?

Was there a natural disaster that impacted you or your business?

Did you rely on the advice of a CPA or IRS employee in making tax decisions?

Were there any circumstances that created substantial financial hardship, to the point where either yourself or your business was close to going bankrupt?

These questions cover all of the IRS reasonable cause criteria to one extent or another, so finding an answer to your personal or business situation that covers one or more of these questions is the key to a successful penalty abatement application.

Writing Your Penalty Abatement Request

You can use Form 843, Claim for Refund and Request for Abatement to apply for relief from penalties. However, as a tax practitioner, I never have, not even once. The reason is simply because the form only has room for about two sentences in order to explain WHY you are requesting the penalties to be removed. Therefore, you're going to end up writing a lengthy letter anyway that gets attached to the Form 843. Because of this, I simply write a letter for my clients that includes all the same information as the Form 843. My typical penalty abatement letter is 3 to 5 pages long, and some are even longer.

The format of a penalty abatement letter is fairly straightforward. When requesting a penalty abatement, I suggest the following format:

Indicate the particular penalty types, tax periods, and penalty amounts that you are requesting to be reduced or removed.

Include a very brief introduction about who you are, where you live, your family size, and what you do. For a business, give a very brief description of your business, what it does, and how it does it.

Provide the background story to the event that caused the tax bills to go unpaid. Be sure to include very specific details, including names, dates, places, events, etc.

After explaining why the taxes weren't paid, explain what actions you took to correct the situation, including an explanation regarding the length of time it took to get the tax situation addressed.

For business taxes, explain why other business expenses were paid when the taxes were not.

Explain the current state of affairs, including the current status of your personal or business finances, and also the status of meeting your current tax obligations and how you've addressed the back tax liabilities

Sign your request under penalties of perjury.

Where To Send Penalty Abatement Requests

If you have or recently had a Revenue Officer assigned to you, send your penalty abatement request to that Revenue Officer.

If you do not have a Revenue Officer: Most of your IRS notices most likely come from one particular IRS service center. Make note of the address of that IRS center, and mail your request their to the attention of "Service Center Penalty Appeals Coordinator".

Penalty Abatement Review Process

Whether it is a Revenue Officer or the service center coordinator that reviews your request, they will make a determination regarding whether they believe your request meets reasonable cause criteria.

If it is determined that your application meets reasonable cause criteria, the person reviewing your request will recommend removal of penalties for certain types and period, based on your circumstances. This recommendation will then be forwarded to a manager for final approval.

If your request is denied, you will be told so in writing. You are entitled to know the exact reason that your request was denied. If you are not supplied with this reason in the initial rejection letter, then you should call or write to that person to request it.

All penalty abatement denials have appeals rights. Requesting appeals consideration of your penalty abatement is covered in the next chapter.

Need Help With Penalties?

If you would like assistance with a penalty abatement application, we have a successful track record of writing applications that work. Contact our office at **(207) 741-2400** for assistance.

Sean T. O'Hare, CPA

Tax Resolution Wrap-up

Tax resolution is a long, challenging journey. It can take many years to resolve unpaid taxes because the balance compounds so quickly with penalties and interest. To make matters worse, the IRS essentially acts like a big bully and stops at nothing to collect money past due. While a tax resolution specialist such as a CTRS will not be able to make your tax woes go away, they can soften the impact significantly.

Because they know and understand the laws and know how to talk to the IRS, they can often get a lot further than a taxpayer working on his own. If you have received a notice from the IRS, your first step should be to find a CTRS to help you through the process. You will want to move quickly and be sure to verify their certification through the American Society of Tax Problem Solvers.

Though it may seem like it at the time, tax troubles are not the end of the world. There are ways to deal with problems, and the more quickly you react, the better the situation will turn out for you. The best strategy is to avoid problems altogether by being completely honest, accurate, and timely in your tax filings. But if you do end up in trouble, this is one area in particular where it is highly recommended to bring in professional assistance.

If you're looking for a qualified tax resolution representative, give me a call at **(207) 741-2400**.

Sean T. O'Hare, CPA

Conclusion

Personal finance begins with an understanding of the basics. From there, you can move on to develop a financial strategy that will help see you through your life comfortably, no matter what your income may be.

Whether you are rich or poor, understanding how to manage your money is crucial to getting along in this world. While money is certainly not something that you want to make your sole focus in life, it does deserve your attention.

Money is about more than having things. In our bustling modern world, money is the barter system. We cannot trade shells and spices and precious metals anymore. Well, you can when the location and circumstances are right, but if you were to try to pay for your groceries with a shell necklace, the cashier would shoot you a dirty look and ask you for cash or a credit card.

One of the most fundamental aspects of personal finance is credit. Your credit rating and your credit profile are at the foundation of everything financial. While you do not have to have a sterling record to be able to participate in the financial system, the more careful you are about managing your credit, the easier it is to thrive. With good credit, you can get a nicer home, borrow money at lower rates, and even get a better job. Good credit is immensely helpful to people who want to start a business. To lenders and financers, it says something positive about your character.

The banking system provides a relatively safe way to store and track your money. Because few employers will pay you in cash, chances are that you are going to have to use the banking system to get paid. Checking and savings accounts are an easy way to keep track of things and usually less expensive than check-cashing services. They are also more secure than hiding cash under a mattress.

Because nobody is going to pay for your retirement, you have to plan for yourself. While most Americans can count on at least a small stipend from Social Security, it is rarely enough to cover all of your expenses.

Retirement plans such as 401(k)s and IRAs are some of the most popular ways to save for retirement. Annuities, life insurance, and other investments can also make up the balance of what is needed to fund your golden years.

Taxes are an unavoidable part of personal finance. If you are an employee, they are taken out of your paycheck. If you run a business, the government is there with its hand out waiting for payment. The penalties for avoiding taxes make it a horrible idea to do anything but pay them. Rather than getting upset about taxes, the best strategy is to plan for them and pay them on time. It is a wise decision to use the services of a qualified tax professional just to make sure that all of your calculations are correct, the correct forms are filed, and that your accounting processes are similar from one year to the next. This is especially relevant if you run a business or have a high income.

Like anything in life, personal finance is easier when it is not a mystery. Unfortunately, few people enter adulthood with the tools and knowledge they need to manage their finances successfully. Lack of knowledge is why there are a lot of young people with high amounts of credit card debt, and a lot of adults who make decent money but never seem to "make it." The lack of education around personal finances also puts people at a disadvantage when it comes to planning for retirement.

Though the modern financial system has its shortcomings, it also offers a lot of benefits as far as personal finances are concerned. When you need a little extra money to cover bills, it is available one way or another. When you need to keep money safe, you can put it in a savings account or safe deposit box. If you want to try your hand at investing, there are a bunch of options!

After reading this book, you should feel better equipped with the basic knowledge needed to manage personal finances going forward. Planning, being proactive, and being realistic are the name of the game. Living within your means and enjoying all that you have will go a long way toward helping you achieve financial freedom!

ABOUT THE AUTHOR

Sean T. O'Hare is a tax resolution expert. He is the founder and CEO of Tax Debt Assistance and O'Hare Associates, CPAs, dedicated to helping individuals with tax debt and tax issue resolutions. He has been a Boston CPA for over 20 years and is known as New England's go-to tax resolution expert.

Sean holds a Master's Degree in Taxation from Thomas College, is a Certified Public Accountant (CPA) as well as an Enrolled Agent (EA). He is also a Certified Tax Resolution Specialist (CTRS), and a National Tax Practice Institute (NTPI) Fellow, and a Personal Financial Specialist (PFS).

Sean maintains offices in Portland, ME, Boston, MA, and Portsmouth, NH. To schedule a consultation via phone or at one of his offices, please call (855) 383-2400.